Next-Level Negotiating

D1316242

Women *at* Work
Inspiring conversations, advancing together

The **HBR WOMEN AT WORK SERIES** spotlights the real challenges and opportunities women experience throughout their careers. With interviews from the popular podcast of the same name and related articles, stories, and research, these books provide inspiration and advice for taking on topics at work like inequity, advancement, and building community. Featuring detailed discussion guides, this series will help you spark important conversations about where we're at and how to move forward.

Books in the series include:

Making Real Connections

Next-Level Negotiating

Speak Up, Speak Out

Taking Charge of Your Career

Thriving in a Male-Dominated Workplace

You, the Leader

Women *at* Work

Inspiring conversations, advancing together

Next-Level Negotiating

Harvard Business Review Press
Boston, Massachusetts

Copyright 2023 Harvard Business School Publishing Corporation
All rights reserved
Printed in the United States of America

10 9 8 7 6 5 4 3 2 1

The web addresses referenced in this book were live and correct at the time of the book's publication but may be subject to change.

Library of Congress Cataloging-in-Publication Data

Names: Harvard Business Review Press, issuing body.
Title: Next-level negotiating.
Other titles: HBR women at work series.
Description: Boston, Massachusetts : Harvard Business Review Press, [2022]
Series: HBR women at work series | Includes index.
Identifiers: LCCN 2022022697 (print) | LCCN 2022022698 (ebook) |
   ISBN 9781647824334 (paperback) | ISBN 9781647824341 (epub)
Subjects: LCSH: Negotiation in business. | Women employees. |
   Success in business. | Psychology, Industrial.
Classification: LCC HD58.6 .N49 2022 (print) | LCC HD58.6 (ebook) |
   DDC
658.4/052--dc23/eng/20220611
LC record available at https://lccn.loc.gov/2022022697
LC ebook record available at https://lccn.loc.gov/2022022698

ISBN: 978-1-64782-433-4
eISBN: 978-1-64782-434-1

The paper used in this publication meets the requirements of the American National Standard for Permanence of Paper for Publications and Documents in Libraries and Archives Z39.48-1992.

CONTENTS

Contents

Every Negotiation Is an Opportunity to Learn and Deepen Relationships

by Amy Gallo, cohost of *Women at Work*

A few years ago, I almost hired someone to negotiate for me. My first book, the *HBR Guide to Dealing with Conflict*, had just come out, and I was starting to give talks and workshops based on it. But every time I spoke to a potential client—a conference organizer or the learning and development lead at a company—I would dread the point in the conversation where we'd discuss fees. I found it awkward and uncomfortable. I hated trying to figure out whether I should name a price or inquire what their budget was first. I hated feeling like my professional value was being debated. I hated knowing that, as a woman, I'd be judged more harshly for advocating for myself. I hated the sinking suspicion that other speakers—even those with a commensurate amount of experience—were getting paid more. And I especially hated finding out that men who were presenting at the same event were indeed commanding higher fees.

So I started talking to speaking agents. When they asked why I wanted someone to represent me, I was clear: *I don't want to negotiate.* One of the potential agents laughed and responded, "I guess even conflict experts hate negotiating."

That was when a light bulb went off. If my goal during my speaking engagements is to help people in the audience learn how to handle difficult conversations productively and professionally, shouldn't I be able to take my own advice?!

I didn't end up signing with a speaker's bureau then. Instead, I decided to endure the awkwardness and the concern that I wasn't doing it right, and I followed the advice I gave in my talks about being clear on what I wanted, keeping that goal in mind, advocating for myself, and establishing boundaries. Five years later, I no longer dread those conversations about fees, but with the publication of my second book, I signed with an agent when the volume of requests just became too much to handle on my own.

Do I approach these negotiations with 100% confidence? Sometimes. Self-doubt and discomfort still creep in on occasion. But now I know how to work through those feelings and even use them to my advantage. Getting better at these conversations has made me more confident and skilled in all negotiations, whether I'm requesting responsibility for a project, saying no to an assignment I don't have bandwidth for, or trying to convince my teenage daughter to clean her room.

I remember hearing professor Ashleigh Shelby Rosette caution women to not "negotiate against themselves" on an episode of the *Women at Work* podcast in season 1 (that was back before I was a cohost, when I was a listener and a fan of the show). By that, she meant that it's not our job to think of all the reasons that our counterparts will say no and downgrade our request or desires before we even get to the negotiation table (something I certainly had been guilty of). It was such valuable guidance, and I took it to heart. I had the privilege of interviewing Ashleigh later and was able to ask her more about the pitfalls to avoid and how to prepare for a negotiation. That interview is chapter 2 in this book.

There are lots of misconceptions about women and negotiation: We're bad at it, we care too much about being empathetic or nice, we see it as a chore and avoid it at all costs. They simply aren't true. These are sweeping generalizations that have been debunked by studies over the last 20-plus years. What *is* true, however, is that women are often penalized for negotiating, as research by Hannah Riley Bowles and Linda Babcock has shown. Advocating for ourselves doesn't align with gender expectations that we will care about others and put their needs first; the threat of losing relationships or being disliked is a real risk.

While the reality that women face additional obstacles (yet again) is depressing, there is hope. By negotiating in a way that is creative and collaborative, we can reach resolutions that meet our needs and those of the other people involved. And we can deepen relationships with those we work with regularly, learning more about their context and goals and sharing our own.

Another misunderstanding about negotiations is that either you can get the results you want, whether that's a higher salary, a better deal, a more manageable workload, *or* you can preserve your relationship with the other person—your manager, a client, or a friend. People assume there's a choice to be made—drive a hard bargain or make a concession to preserve the relationship. But, in most negotiations, you can do both—stand firm *and* maintain your relationships. In fact, becoming a more confident, consistent, and effective negotiator can improve your connections with others at work, something I write about in my second book, *Getting Along: How to Work with Anyone (Even Difficult People)*. Rather than harming your relationships with those you frequently interact or negotiate with, you're likely to garner respect when people see you as someone who can make the case for a budget increase, close a deal with a customer, advocate for your own career development and pay, and resolve differences before they escalate into unhealthy conflicts.

One important note: This book is not a primer or a step-by-step guide that takes you from preparation to closing the deal. (If that's what you need, I highly recommend checking out the *HBR Guide to Negotiating*.) *Next-Level Negotiating* is a collection of some of our best articles and advice, selected to help anyone who is interested in understanding more about negotiation through a gender lens and supporting themselves or others in improving their skills in this area. We know from the podcast that this is something many of our listeners and readers want—to feel less awkward and more self-assured in asking for and getting what they want, whether they're resolving a conflict with a customer, convincing colleagues to change a policy, agreeing on a project budget, or settling on the specifics of a new job.

The articles and interviews in this collection outline tactics that work, offer advice for putting them in practice, and provide guidance on what to do when you're struggling to get to a resolution, all while paying attention to the nuances of how gender affects how we're perceived and treated. There's also a specific section on negotiating jobs and raises, since that is one of the most common—and often most fraught—negotiations that we engage in.

I'm guessing that you picked up this book because this is a skill that you want to get better at—whether you already enjoy negotiating or dread it, like I used to. No matter where you stand now, putting in the time and effort to get better at tough conversations will hone your interpersonal skills, improve your creative reasoning abilities, and ensure that you and your career move forward, rather than stall out. I know this book will help—not just at work, but in your personal life as well.

Prepare Yourself

1

How Women Can Get What They Want in a Negotiation

by Suzanne de Janasz and Beth Cabrera

Tara, an MD/PhD who works for a large public university, contacted one of us (Suzanne) a few weeks after participating in a negotiation workshop she ran, wanting to share some positive news about successfully negotiating an 11% pay increase. A faculty member for six years, she had come to learn that she was not only underpaid but also had a higher teaching and clinic load than others in her group. She, like many women, accepted her job offer without negotiating.

How common is Tara's situation? Research suggests that 20% of women never negotiate at all.[1] A woman who opts not to negotiate her starting salary upon graduation will forgo an average of $7,000 the first year and will lose between $650,000 and $1 million over the course of a

45-year career.[2] Why would women leave money on the table? There are several factors. When selecting metaphors for the process of negotiation, men pick "winning a ballgame," while women pick "going to the dentist."[3] Expectations drive behavior. If women see negotiation as a chore, they either don't negotiate or do so in ways that can hurt the outcome. There is also the (very real) fear, backed by research, that negotiating may come at the cost of being disliked.[4]

The good news is that negotiating skills can be enhanced. Based on a growing body of research on gender in negotiations, combined with burgeoning research on positivity and mindfulness, we offer five strategies that can help women both choose to engage and perform more effectively in negotiations.

Preparing Fully

In general, people don't like doing what they believe they're not good at and often opt not to engage in activities in which failure is likely. The more we fear something, the longer and more fervently we stay away from it, and the greater power we give it—a vicious cycle. Investing effort in preparing for a negotiation—knowing what you want and why, thinking through acceptable alternatives, and developing specific strategies for being persuasive—can significantly increase your confidence and competence.[5] Moreover, thinking through other desirable outcomes or alternatives will give you flexibility and comfort, knowing that you don't have to take whatever is offered.

Once Tara started gathering salary data from Glassdoor and other reliable sources, she began to understand her worth, and she committed to taking steps to achieve parity. Compared with men, women are less likely to be aware of, and are more uncomfortable expressing, their value.[6] Tara's preparation helped her overcome this barrier. Going into a salary negotiation with data, along with a planned and persuasive explanation of achievements and capabilities that warrant a higher salary, can greatly increase one's confidence in and expectation of a successful outcome. Visualizing or practicing (by role-playing, for example) the negotiation in advance further embeds the skills and cognitive and behavioral readiness for the negotiation, increasing the chances of success even more.[7]

Cultivating Positive Emotions

Positive emotions can help women negotiate more effectively by increasing their willingness to seek mutually beneficial solutions and improving their ability to engage in creative thinking to identify a wider range of options. People in positive moods prefer collaboration over competition.[8] By cultivating positive moods, women will be more likely to work to achieve integrative gains—asserting their needs while encouraging the other party to do the same.[9] This will increase the probability of reaching a mutually satisfying, optimal agreement.[10]

Research demonstrates that people experiencing positive affect show patterns of thought that are more flexible, unusual, integrative, and open than those whose affect is negative or neutral. Thinking of a joyful memory helped students perform better on a standardized test, and boosting the moods of medical students by giving them candy improved their accuracy and creativity.[11] Prior to a negotiation, women can use positive priming (thinking about something positive or engaging in a joyful activity) to increase positive emotions, resulting in greater creativity, openness, and willingness to collaborate, all of which are essential to successful negotiation.

Boosting Emotional Intelligence

Emotional intelligence involves an awareness of one's own emotions and the emotions of others. Being more aware of her emotions can boost a woman's confidence in negotiating. It lowers the intensity of emotions and reduces reactivity by providing a moment in which to consider how best to respond.[12] This emotional control can help women negotiate more successfully and give them greater self-assurance, especially in difficult situations.

With increased confidence, women will be more likely to assert their needs. Confidence may also reduce anxiety about negotiating, which women experience to a greater degree than men.[13] This can increase the likelihood that women choose to enter a negotiation to begin with. And a greater awareness of the emotions of others during a negotiation can help women better understand their needs and interests, which can make it easier to find integrative solutions.

Emotional intelligence can be developed through mindfulness. Mindfulness is paying attention to the present moment—what's going on in the world around you, as well as your thoughts and feelings. Being mindful can, therefore, increase your emotional awareness. One of the best ways for women to become more mindful is to practice meditation. Focusing your attention on something like your breath, and bringing it back each time your mind wanders, even for a few minutes a day, builds your ability to stay focused. It has also been shown to decrease the emotional reactivity of the amygdala, which is activated when facing situations perceived to be dangerous, overwhelming, or threatening.[14] (For more on using mindfulness during negotiations, see chapter 10.)

Negotiating Communally

While male (or masculine) negotiators may win the battle but lose the war because of their competitiveness and unsympathetic approach to relationships, women may suffer on both accounts—issues and relationships—because focusing on their own needs causes others to view them as bossy and aggressive.[15] One way to overcome this challenge is to reframe a negotiation as though you are negotiating on behalf of a group or other individuals.[16] For example, a woman who negotiates for increased resources to enhance the quality or the productivity of a department that has been stretched by downsizing and low morale will be seen as collaborative, not aggressive. Research demonstrates that women who adopt a "relational" or "I-we" strategy, in which they show concern for the other person's perspective, can minimize the social cost of negotiation.[17]

The ability to reframe the negotiation—even one with the goal of increasing one's total compensation—into one where the other party also benefits is particularly important for women. The collaborative or communal mindset—enhanced by preparation and a positive mood—can help a woman find an I-we strategy that is good not just for her but also for the company or for some larger cause that she and the other party both believe in. Considering the interests of the other party and suggesting integrative solutions can boost the likelihood of success. For example, instead of saying, "Getting an MBA is important for my development as a manager," frame your ask as a win-win: "With the additional financial and managerial skills I'll gain in an MBA program, I'll be able to assist in or lead more complex tasks or projects, enabling you to focus on more strategic and high-level priorities."

Negotiating a Package

People from other cultures negotiate differently. Whereas Americans and Germans prefer a linear, one-issue-at-a-time approach, the French prefer a more holistic approach and will move back and forth on issues that other negotiators may have believed were long since settled. While the latter approach might appear confusing or chaotic to some, the multi-issue or package approach to negotiating enables women to be viewed as less competitive or aggressive. When there is one issue, the negotiation is more likely to be seen as adversarial: win or lose. However, when multiple issues are considered, women can be more collaborative and problem-solving: "If I give you this, then you can give me that." This will help them to be seen in a more positive way.

In the case of salary negotiation, look at the total compensation package, which might include paid time off, the hiring of an assistant, or a commuting allowance—all of which have monetary value—as opposed to salary alone. Whereas a package offers opportunities to trade off issues that may have different value to each party, a singular salary focus can lead to an impasse (neither party budges), win-lose distributiveness (one party out-maneuvers the other), or compromise (both parties give up some of what they want). In some situations, salary ranges can be fixed, whereas performance bonuses, housing allowances, and other forms of compensation are not. Rather than saying, "My minimum salary expectation is $120,000," try, "I'd be willing to consider a salary that is below my minimum if we can agree on the total compensation package. In addition to my eligibility for year-end bonuses, I'd like to discuss administrative support, relocation assistance, and the possibility of two months' rental in a furnished apartment, given my 800-mile relocation." Back up your request with some data gathering of norms in the industry, the region, or, better still, the company.

Whether negotiating salary, company resources, or complex multiyear contracts, women need to overcome challenges with respect to their motivation, confidence, and the expectations of others. By preparing effectively and enhancing their negotiation skills, they'll increase their ability to come up with creative solutions that work better for everyone involved.

Adapted from content posted on hbr.org, August 17, 2018 (product #H04HIO).

2

Understanding the Negotiation Process

A conversation with Marisa Mauro
and Ashleigh Shelby Rosette

Whether we're negotiating a salary, a deal with a supplier, or flexible work arrangements, we need to go in prepared. Otherwise we risk not getting the things we want and need. But what are the most important factors to consider ahead of time? When, if ever, should we reveal to the other party our priorities—and terms we absolutely can't agree to? And because advocating and bargaining for ourselves, our employees, and our businesses can feel so personal, how do we manage the emotions that come up?

Like many of us, Marisa Mauro built her career by negotiating. She started a one-woman business, Ploughgate Creamery, after mastering the craft of making cheese in small batches. Over the next few years, she grew the business and gained recognition, winning a first-place award from the American Cheese Society. But the facility where she rented space burned down, so Mauro took a break and got a job waitressing. One day she learned that the Vermont Land Trust had opened applications to farmers interested in buying 50 acres of land and the century-old defunct farm on it at less than market price. Mauro submitted a business plan to make butter there that the Land Trust accepted. But before she could put that plan into action, she had to formalize it legally by creating a conservation easement. Next, she negotiated for all the labor, equipment, and raw materials needed to get the farm functioning again. As a small-business owner, she's never stopped negotiating. It's an everyday practice. But she hadn't really stopped to name, analyze, and appreciate the underlying principles.

Marisa Mauro spoke with *Women at Work* host Amy Gallo and Ashleigh Shelby Rosette, a Duke University professor whose research centers on negotiations.

AMY GALLO: Marisa, what types of negotiations are you engaged in regularly?

MARISA MAURO: As a small-business owner, I have to be involved in many different levels of negotiation with different demographics of people. I have to get my product to market through distribution. There are many ways that works, with pricing and logistics. Then there are the farmers I buy cream from directly and the farmers that also lease my land for other agricultural purposes. And I also negotiate with my employees.

AMY: Can you share an example of a negotiation you went through?

MARISA: The dairy farmers that I purchase cream from told me they would have a shortage in the coming months and were unsure of a solution. I called a meeting to bring us all together. Building relationships is important to me in running a small business. When I went to meet with the farmers, I baked a pie, brought butter, and we all sat around a table. That was a great way to break the ice with them. In my mind, a contract would have been ideal, but it's not always possible for the nature and scale of my business. The first thing one of the farmers said was, "I bet you were hoping for a contract." So, I knew that was immediately off the table. I asked them to explain to me the inner workings of the processing plant. And I asked questions about the volumes other customers were getting, and about the staffing and equipment that they use. I learned that they needed an additional piece of equipment to solve the issue. I said, "There it is. I can help." And I was able to source the equipment and keep us on track. It wasn't about prices; it was about ensuring that I could get the volume of cream I needed to hit the sales goals that make my company viable.

ASHLEIGH SHELBY ROSETTE: You've highlighted some really important ideas. One, that negotiation occurs in phases. And the phases can be short or long—it depends on the type of negotiation and the goal (see table 2-1). So, for you, this is a long, continued relationship. That first phase of building rapport can last five minutes or months,

TABLE 2-1

The negotiation process

Every negotiation involves different players, interests, and goals. Despite those differences, most negotiations follow the four phases shown here. Once you understand the process and strategies for each phase, you can adapt your approach to individual situations.

Phases of negotiation	What's involved
1. Prepare to negotiate.	• Identify the type and scope of the negotiation. • Establish and improve your position. • Assess the other party's position. • Identify the zone of possible agreement.
2. Conduct the negotiation, including offers and counteroffers.	• Set the stage and tone. • Use your strategies. • Continually evaluate what's happening.
3. Finalize the agreement.	• Prevent errors and manage your emotions. • Handle impasses. • Close the deal. • Evaluate the outcome.
4. Fulfill the agreement.	• Carry out the agreement. • Meet your commitments. • Capture and share what you learned.

Source: Excerpted from "Understand Negotiation," Harvard ManageMentor, https://hbp.myhbp.org/hmm12/content/negotiating/understand_negotiation.html.

just to make sure you have a certain level of trust before the transaction can even take place. So, you recognized that and, most importantly, the farmers communicated that up front, which helped to manage the process quite well. Had you talked for two hours thinking that you'd have a deal at the end, that might have been very frustrating for you. But because they initially said, "Look, let us just tell you about our process. There's probably not going to be a deal today." That allows you to say, "OK, now the pressure is off. We're just sharing information. We're just getting to know each other." Because of the rapport that you were attempting to develop, they were willing to share with you and be vulnerable. Then you were able to find a way that you could work together, something that probably didn't hurt you very much, but helped them a lot. And you gave the basis for that transaction that comes later on. So, the first phase can be short or long. You recognized the goal and diagnosed that ahead of time.

AMY: I like this idea of phases, Ashleigh. It sounds like the first phase was the baking of the pie. She planned for this conversation by thinking about the connection with the farmers. What is the correct preparation? Do we always need to bake pies?

ASHLEIGH: A frequent mantra that I use is that a good negotiator is a prepared negotiator. And preparation begins before the negotiation. Marisa thought about what she could do before they sat at the table. Another good way to prepare involves a planning document, where you actually write down the things that are important to you. What are your goals? What are your alternatives? How are you going to begin this negotiation? A good planning document can help minimize your anxiety, increase your confidence, and minimize gaffes at the negotiation table. It's a written record of some of the vital issues. Thinking about these issues before the negotiation puts you in a better place to manage the process. You may even map it out. In this first meeting, we want to accomplish this; in phase two, we want to accomplish that.

MARISA: If I wanted to create a document for future negotiations, what questions do you suggest I include?

ASHLEIGH: First we diagnose the type of negotiation. Is this distributive, where I'm trying to get the most for myself? Is it integrative, where we're both trying to get something and create value? Once you diagnose the type of negotiation, then that's going to dictate the types of questions to consider. What are the issues on the table? List all the issues and then rank them. Which ones are the most important to me? Which ones would I be willing to give on? In a perfect world, this is my ideal target. What's the least that I'm willing to accept? If I don't get a deal, what am I going to do? Keeping an eye on that alternative is important. You need to know when you want to walk away, to make sure that you don't take something sub-par in this negotiation. The stronger that alternative is, the better the negotiation tends to be. Because you have a really strong alternative, you push really hard in that negotiation, because you're not going to take anything less. But think about these things before you negotiate and not in the middle of it. (See table 2-2.)

Also focus on the opposing party. What is their goal? If you think about what your alternative is, what will

TABLE 2-2

Identify the type of negotiation: Single- versus multiple-issue negotiations

Before you begin bargaining, you need to know what kind of negotiation you are engaging in. This knowledge will influence your strategy and the choices you make. The two main types are single-issue negotiation, also known as distributive or win-lose negotiation, and multiple-issue negotiation, also known as integrative or win-win negotiation.

Characteristic	Single-issue negotiations	Multiple-issue negotiations
Number of issues involved	One	Several
Outcome	Win-lose	Win-win
Motivation	Individual gain	Joint and individual gain
Interests	Opposed	Different value and priority placed on issues
Duration	Short term	Short or long term
Ability to make trade-offs	Not flexible	Flexible
Solution	Not creative	Creative

Source: Excerpted from "Prepare to Negotiate," Harvard ManageMentor, https://hbp
.myhbp.org/hmm12/content/negotiating/prepare_to_negotiate.html.

cause them to walk away? What are their most important issues? Use the negotiation process to go through a diagnostic to see what you thought about ahead of time. Because they're trying to guess what is the least amount that you're trying to get, and you're trying to get what is the most amount that they're trying to pay. Gathering that information, thinking about that whole process of all those issues, helps you determine what the bargaining zone is so that you end up coming to a favorable agreement.

MARISA: Would you say my negotiation with the farmers was an integrative negotiation?

ASHLEIGH: No, you took a distributive negotiation and made it integrative by adding an additional issue. You were able to uncover that additional issue by developing rapport with them, such that they were willing to trust you and share information. Sometimes when you don't have that rapport and trust, people will keep their problems close to the vest, because they think that you might take that information, exploit it, and use it against them. But instead, you took something that was initially about getting a deal to move your business forward, and you made it much bigger than that, so you weren't claiming value. You were actually creating value for both of you. You turned a distributive negotiation into an integrative negotiation, and you did that exceptionally well.

AMY: What about the role of relationships? It sounds like Marisa prioritized her relationship with the farmers. Is that something that most people should do in a negotiation?

ASHLEIGH: It depends on the nature of the negotiation. One of the characteristics of the negotiation that Marisa has described is the notion of recurrence. In a long-term or recurring negotiation, relationships are important, especially as circumstances change. In this situation, circumstances changed in that there was going to be a shortage of cream. The relationship allows for trust and the sharing of information. Imagine what would have happened if you hadn't developed that relationship. You would be without your cream. You wouldn't be able to continue your business. But you were able to do so because of that relationship. In integrative negotiations, that notion of trust is really important. But some negotiations are distributive in nature, where it's all about claiming value. If you're going to buy a car, you're never going to see the salesperson again, and you're just trying to get a good deal, so the relationship isn't quite as important.

AMY: Marisa, thinking about the anxiety that many of us feel in negotiations, what part causes you the most concern?

MARISA: A lot of times I'm pretty direct with people. Sometimes I come off as aggressive, and then the other party shuts down. But it's just my nature. Sometimes I have anxiety around that when I see the other party shutting down. Because I'm an entrepreneur and fast paced, and I see opportunity, I get really excited and passionate. But not everybody's at that level. I don't have time for the fluff around it. So sometimes, if I'm trying to solve a problem, or I'm trying to negotiate, I want to just hear the facts, not all the details.

AMY: That is such an interesting conundrum: How do I get through this negotiation as quickly and efficiently as possible, while also not damaging the relationship? That makes me think about the research around gender and negotiations, and how women are often seen as pushy or bossy when they're advocating for themselves. Basically, they're penalized for being assertive. Any advice for how Marisa can think about taking the right approach to her style in negotiations?

ASHLEIGH: Marisa, you were saying that you're very direct. But what I heard you describe is that you were utilizing what you call "the fluff" very effectively. Your communication style may be very direct, but you really do understand how to build relationships. Those things don't necessarily have to work against each other. The notion of being assertive and direct is something that as women we tend to have to manage because those perceptions and those stereotypes exist. Not everyone will perceive these as negative, but some will, which means that we have to manage those perceptions if we're going to develop relationships effectively and ultimately get the type of deal that we want. When you think about being direct, you have to also step back and say, "What exactly does that mean? When I say that I am direct, I'm being direct in what way and in what capacity? Does that mean that I'm asking specific questions? Well, that's not a bad thing, right?" And once you have established those relationships, people give you the benefit of the doubt. You have rapport, and they think, "Oh, well, that's just Marisa, and she's very direct."

If you don't have that rapport and people don't know you, and you come out with guns blazing, that's going to put them on their heels saying, "Hold up. Wait a minute." So even though we want to be direct, we have to recognize how we're being perceived and manage that. If you feel as though that other person is on their heels, you probably need to alter your communication style and pause to see what they're thinking and how they're reacting, as opposed to just kind of going and going. It's all about managing that process.

So, thinking about that planning document, if you're direct and know you're negotiating with someone else who is direct, this should be fine. But if you're direct and negotiating with someone who needs to take their time, that relationship is important. They want to get to know you a bit better. It is in your best interest not to circumvent that process, because that could be detrimental at the negotiation table. Preparing for the negotiation is not just about the issues, but it also involves thinking about who that person is on the opposite side of the table. I am not saying don't be authentic, don't be yourself. I'm simply saying that we have to manage this process such that we put our best selves forward and people perceive us in the way that we intend, not in a way that could be adverse to the negotiation outcome.

AMY: Marisa, you're being direct and people shut down. When she sees that in her negotiation counterparts, how does she change tack in that moment?

ASHLEIGH: There are numerous strategies. Sometimes take a break and then come back and reset. Another alternative is to label the process, saying, "Did I come on too strong there? If I did, that wasn't my intention. Tell me what you're thinking about what I just said." By disentangling the personality from the content of what has been said and labeling the process, you can easily do that. That way, they're responding to the issue—the content of what you said—not the manner in which you may have delivered it.

If for some reason you're emotionally entangled, or you're communicating in such an assertive way that it can derail the effectiveness of the negotiation, then that might be the time to bring in a third party or an agent to talk on your behalf. Because if you can't disentangle the emotion, assertiveness, or style from the issue, that can be very difficult to do.

MARISA: I really like the idea of labeling the process. That adds a personal touch, which is the way I like to operate. I'm the owner of a small business, and all my negotiations feel so personal. Do you have any advice on how to keep my emotions in check with this level of intimacy?

ASHLEIGH: On one hand, communicating emotions can have a positive effect, because it can convey how passionate you are about certain issues. So, to get what we want, we have to ask for what we want. People have to understand our preferences. Emotions can be a fantastic way to communicate what is or is not important to you. On the other hand, communicating emotions can have a negative effect, as it can hinder your ability to make good decisions and undermine your credibility. Make sure that emotions do not become integral to the decision-making process and the negotiation process, and if they are involved, that they remain tangential. One way to do that is to distinguish feeling your emotions from conveying your emotions. Sometimes we can't do that. But at the negotiation table, what you feel does not always have to equate with what you say. Negotiators are in a constant state of managing emotions. Being in touch with your own emotions and perceiving others' emotions can be an extremely important part of the negotiation process. And if this is something that people tend to struggle with, they should learn about emotional intelligence and the five steps associated with it.

People have brought emotional intelligence into the negotiation arena. The notion of self-awareness, self-regulation, self-motivation, empathy, and ultimately building great social skills at the negotiation table are the steps involved in demonstrating our emotional intelligence. That can be a way such that we feel our emotions, but don't necessarily convey them. Conveying emotions is not always negative, but there is balance. So, for example, some of our research says it's not just about the emotions that you feel naturally, but you can use emotion strategically at the negotiations table. So we know that when we're in a positive mood, then we're more creative. But we know when there's a distributive negotiation, we may need to be a bit more rational, more poker-faced. Sometimes when we're trying to claim value, and we've been at the table for a long time, we need to throw a little negative emotion in there. There are so many layers to emotions at the negotiation table that it really should be one of those things that we think about when we're preparing for the negotiation. (See section 3, "Manage Your Emotions.")

So if you're thinking, "This is my baby, this is personal," know what your triggers are. Practice how to react to those triggers. If you know that when somebody says this, it's going to make you react in a certain way, and if that's not the way you want to react, then you probably need to practice responding in a different way so that when those triggers come up, you're prepared for them. When you're feeling an emotion, you choose whether or not it's in your best interest to convey that emotion.

AMY: I love this idea of familiarizing yourself with your own triggers. For me, it's when someone insinuates that I'm not being fair, because that's something I really pride myself on. So, if someone I'm in a negotiation with starts to act as if I'm being unreasonable or disregarding their feelings or thoughts, I get really upset. Do you have any specific tips on how to practice responding, especially when we know we get really emotional around those specific issues?

ASHLEIGH: What you just described is a sole focus on self and not considering the opposing party. You have to recognize that fairness is a perception. And what you perceive to be fair may not be what the other party perceives to be fair. "Fair" can be based on need. It can be based on precedent, inequality, inequity, things of that nature. When you think about your trigger, step back from it and say, "How might my definition of fairness be different from their definition of fairness?" And perhaps you should incorporate that into your process. Say, "This is something that's really important to me. I define fairness as this. How do you see fairness? Do you see fairness in the same way in which I do?" So, if you know that's going to be a trigger, design that in your negotiation process up front. Thinking about those things and addressing them can go a long way to making sure that those triggers don't derail your negotiation process.

AMY: How do you decide at what point to reveal your interests or your position to the other party?

ASHLEIGH: It depends on the type of negotiation you're engaging in. Whether to reveal and what to reveal is not a simple yes-no decision. It usually depends on the situation and the type of negotiation that you find yourself in. Many negotiators' initial response or inclination is to reveal as little as possible so as not to be taken advantage of or exploited by the opposing party. If we step back and think about that negotiation tactic to reveal as little as possible, it is somewhat counterintuitive to the ultimate goal in the negotiation. If the goal is to get a deal that is favorable to you and your circumstances, you eventually have to share the information. That's the opposite of keeping things secret. If we don't reveal our preferences and priorities, we may not get them. If we think about why we feel the need to hold our information close to the vest, it usually derives from the lack of trust that we have toward the other party. And in turn, the lack of trust that they have for us.

One way to build trust is to share information. Usually the norm is reciprocity; they will be relieved, and they will start sharing. This is not always the case. There is a Russian proverb, famous during the Reagan era: "Trust, but verify." Use the same tool of sharing information and reciprocity, but don't share something big. Share something little. Then usually the person will share something little with you. Now, if they didn't get the memo that the norm is reciprocity, you've got to label the process—"I just shared something with you. Can you share something with me?" Then you hope they share. Ultimately you start understanding people's preferences and priorities. So, if you have trust, share information. If you don't have trust, find a way to start building that trust. Maybe you need to have that Russian proverb in the back of your mind.

MARISA: Would it be good to just say the goal out of the gate? Like, my goal is X.

ASHLEIGH: Yes. If you don't have any reason to believe that they are going to exploit you or utilize any information against you, and if you don't think that they would perceive your sharing as weakness, then yes, share. Ask for what you want up front and be direct about it. Ask for what you really want, not for what you would be willing to settle for.

Asking for what you want at the end of the negotiation wastes a lot of time talking about things that are completely irrelevant to you or you don't necessarily care about. If it's something important, give yourself time to talk about it. What would have happened in your negotiation with the farmers had they not told you that they couldn't afford the equipment? If they had waited until the very end, when you're about to walk out the door, saying, "Well, you know, it really is this." Would that have been the most effective use of the time that you spent with them? Probably not.

Adapted from "The Essentials: Negotiating Strategically," Women at Work *podcast, season 7, bonus episode, May 24, 2021.*

3

Stop Overlooking Opportunities to Negotiate

by Suzanne de Janasz

During a workshop for mid- to senior-level career women, I posed the following scenario:

While in your favorite department store, you spot a very attractive pair of "professional" shoes. You happen to know that starting tomorrow, all ladies' shoes will be 30% off. What would you do?

Anne raised her hand confidently and responded, "I'd come back tomorrow." Pivoting quickly, I asked, "What if you're leaving tomorrow morning for a weeklong business trip?" She then responded with "Um . . . maybe I'd see if I could order them online tomorrow at the sale price?"

It's true: not everyone is motivated by a sale price. Similar low-stakes negotiations—like asking your cable company for a better rate or asking for a discount when offering to pay cash—may sometimes not seem worth the effort. However, what if the discomfort you feel around asking for a discount is just the tip of the iceberg? What if the fear of rejection—of the request itself or of you personally—is keeping you from negotiating for anything in the first place? And what if ignoring or avoiding most low-stakes negotiation opportunities is keeping you from feeling confident and competent when approaching more high-stakes negotiations?

If fear is keeping you from negotiating, it's time to start using everyday encounters to practice, so you can build your confidence and competence for higher-stakes negotiations.

Recognizing Opportunities to Negotiate

Most books and articles about negotiation focus on how to prepare or offer strategies for engaging effectively. What these resources fail to address is whether individuals recognize negotiation opportunities in the first place. The ability to recognize an opportunity depends on your perspective and your experience, as well as your culture, role models, and goals. When shopping in a department store, most U.S. consumers see prices as fixed—not open for bargaining. That's less the case when shopping in a flea market, where many items don't have price tags and sellers expect that some shoppers will attempt to haggle for a better price. Beyond commercial opportunities (since not all negotiations involve money, services, or goods), what exactly *is* a negotiation opportunity? It can range anywhere from a disagreement with a neighbor, to the allocation of household chores, to your eligibility for a bonus at work. Consider asking yourself the following questions about situations you encounter in your everyday life:

- Is this situation fair? Are others being offered better compensation, or do they benefit from fewer responsibilities, more resources, a bonus, or a better (cheaper, faster) deal?

- Do I deserve a better or more fair outcome than I have been offered? If someone were to offer this to me now, would I hesitate to accept it?

- Am I feeling uneasy or hesitant about the situation or offer? Would a more confident version of me make a request to get a better or more fair outcome?

Tactical advice about negotiating isn't useful if you fail to recognize or engage in negotiation opportunities. To make matters worse, women negotiate only about 25% as often as men do, and about 20% of all women never negotiate at all.[1] While some women worry about being perceived as aggressive, others might ignore an opportunity to negotiate due to the stress associated with a potential conflict. Many are simply too conflict-avoidant, and others lack confidence in their ability to influence the outcome.

Evaluating Whether to Engage in a Negotiation

Keep in mind that not all opportunities are worth engaging in. The cost-versus-benefit calculus (relative to both the situation and the relationship) simply might not add up. Going back to the shoe example: If the shoes are $100, with the potential for a $30 savings, you might think, "Hmmm, I can come back tomorrow and save $30, or I can pay the $100 now and not have to ask the salesperson an uncomfortable question (such as, 'Excuse me, but is there a way you can give me the 30% discount today? I'm heading out of town tomorrow, and it would be great to get these shoes for the price that others will pay for them in less than 24 hours')." In this evaluation, avoiding the discomfort— and the time such a conversation might take—might be worth $30 for some people. But note that in this example, one is considering the negotiation and making a *choice* about it, as opposed to avoiding the situation altogether.

Evaluating nonmonetary issues can be a bit more complicated. Imagine that you share an apartment with a close friend, and from the beginning, you gravitated toward doing most of the cleaning, cooking, and laundry. When the two of you moved in, you assumed that she would look after herself. She would thank you from time to time, but her perceived laziness has resulted in your growing resentment. You choose not to say anything, afraid of stirring up trouble, but continue doing the majority of the housework. Hints don't work, and the occasional request is met with defensiveness or empty promises to help.

You ask yourself: *Is this fair? Do I deserve to be in a more equitable situation? Is this a negotiation opportunity? Or is this the way things are and I'm going to have to accept this inequitable situation until the lease ends or I move out?* Factoring in individual preferences and comfort levels, one might choose not to negotiate, even when doing so could make a positive difference. But the more you ignore conflictual situations that could be improved with negotiation, the more you give such conflicts power over you. That chore allocation discussion you avoided today might evolve into next week's avoided promotion or raise discussion. The first missed opportunity may result in the degradation of a relationship; the second may result in a serious loss of future earnings. When you consider that a $7,000 starting salary difference over a 43-year career (ages 22–65) adds up to $649,000 (assuming a 3% annual increase), it's clear it's *very* worthwhile to negotiate.

By being mindful about recognizing and evaluating potential negotiation opportunities—weighing the financial, emotional, moral, or psychological trade-offs—you not only put yourself in a position to strategically approach how to negotiate for what you deserve (such as money, recognition, equitable treatment), you also open the door to even better outcomes. You'll learn to improve relationships by working through conflicts. And you'll build a stronger negotiation muscle that will serve you well in higher-stakes negotiations.

Adapted from "We Often Overlook Opportunities to Negotiate," on hbr.org, August 26, 2021 (product #H06JIR).

Negotiate on Your Own Terms

4

Three Common Challenges Women Face in Negotiations

by Mara Olekalns, Ruchi Sinha, and Carol T. Kulik

S mall negotiations are woven through the fabric of our everyday working lives. Managers negotiate to secure resources for their teams, create new positions, or retain existing ones. Employees negotiate to gain more flexible work arrangements, access development opportunities, or define new roles. We use negotiations to help ourselves and our team members and to manage our work as we move toward our goals.

My colleagues and I examined how women experience these everyday negotiations in a field study we conducted.[1] We interviewed 84 women about a significant negotiation that they had been through in the previous year. Our interviewees worked in metropolitan cities, primarily in large organizations with more than 500 employees, and most frequently in health (23%) or government (21%). The majority (81%) had an undergraduate qualification, and their ages ranged from 29 to 64 years. In their interviews, they told us what the negotiation was about, who they negotiated with, and how the negotiation affected their relationship with the other person.

Twenty-two of the women told us about their experience negotiating pay or promotions, but many also talked about the smaller negotiations with coworkers and managers that punctuate their workdays. Other than pay and promotion, the three most common kinds of negotiations were for:

- **Work resources:** to gain support for a new position within the organization, restructure their team, change reporting lines, extend a handover period, or obtain a system upgrade

- **Professional development:** to attend conferences, reduce workdays in order to study, or become involved in higher-level executive meetings

- **Work-life balance:** to adjust work arrangements, restructure a position to fit their family needs, return to work after maternity leave, or request phased retirement

To conclude the interviews, we asked each woman to describe a challenging moment in the negotiation, and around half of the respondents, what advice they would give to other women before a negotiation.

Many of the women talked about negotiation as if it is a battlefield on which a lack of information or clarity on what you (or others) want is a disadvantage. Because of this, they stressed the need to develop core negotiation competencies, such as the ability to plan thoroughly and set goals beforehand. They also talked about the pitfalls of being too aggressive (or not aggressive enough), the challenge of recovering from negative feedback, and the importance of recognizing and taking advantage of opportunities to negotiate.[2]

Based on these concerns, we identified three unique challenges women face during negotiations:

- Balancing self-advocacy and communality

- Managing difficult emotions

- Overcoming interpersonal resistance

Through our research, we have identified evidence-based recommendations to help you develop new skills and build the confidence and resilience you need to overcome them.

Challenge #1: Balancing Self-Advocacy and Communality

The women we interviewed were often reluctant to self-advocate for their career advancement in negotiations.[3] Many told us that just having the confidence to ask for more was challenging.[4] Their reluctance may come from a well-founded fear that if they do ask, they would incur backlash. Research shows that women who initiate negotiations come across as pushy, unlikable, and undesirable team members, and the women in our study expressed their discomfort in creating this impression.[5]

Sasha, a 39-year-old manager in the government sector, told us, "Getting to the point is one thing, but being very demanding and aggressive is another—and it isn't seen as favorable." Jen, a compliance and quality manager, agreed. "I had to basically point out that I manage people better than my male colleague . . . which goes against every part of what I would have liked to do," she said. Sue, a senior manager in the health industry, confirmed this sentiment, saying, "As women, we don't have great role models when it comes to standing up for ourselves. We tend to put the needs of others before our own."

How can you overcome the challenge?

For women, effective self-advocacy requires a balancing act. They often need to come across as neither too assertive nor too caring. To achieve this balance, women are often advised to harness gender stereotypes by overtly displaying warmth and concern for others during negotiations.[6] But this strategy can backfire when the woman appears overly accommodating, and in many cases, acting out of character can increase her stress and anxiety.

You will be more effective if you balance your displays of warmth and assertiveness during negotiations. We suggest you first show that you understand the needs of the other person and then make a more assertive, self-advocating ask. Open a negotiation by laying out the broader issue from the other perspective or by showing how your ask will benefit both you and your team. For example, you might frame the ask for an additional staff member as a resource that will help your team perform more efficiently (rather than help you personally), or you might frame a salary increase as fair compensation given your contributions to the team (rather than as an individual want).[7] A carefully worded ask will help you manage the tension between self-advocacy and communality.

Challenge #2: Managing Difficult Emotions

Negotiations can stir up a variety of emotions in many people, regardless of their gender. But in our study, many women expressed feeling reluctant, anxious, and worried before starting a negotiation because they feared it might end poorly.[8]

Our respondents spoke to the challenge of managing frustration, anger, and hurt during and after these conversations. One woman recalled a negotiation she had with her long-standing work partner. During their discussion, she encountered resistance and responded with anger. "When the negotiation didn't go well," she said, "I became angry. We got in a big fight, if you want to call it that." Because anger is the one emotion that women are not expected to express, she likely ended up doing more harm to the relationship than good. Another interviewee said the worst part about negotiating was becoming emotional during the conversation, and feeling hurt after. Several others discussed how failure at the end of a negotiation created negative emotions that blocked them from following up and making their asks again.

Drawing on their experiences, women identified the ability to distance themselves from their emotions as a necessary skill for being more effective. When giving advice, a few suggested that being less emotionally attached to a specific outcome, and adopting a task orientation instead, might be the answer.

How can you overcome the challenge?

Before the negotiation, one strategy in particular can reduce anticipatory anxiety. Harness your stress and use it to your advantage through defensive pessimism, which is when someone experiencing anxiety lowers their expectations and invests their energy in simulating different ways an interaction could unfold.[9] For example, if you assume that the negotiation will not unfold smoothly, you will be better prepared for any resistance you may encounter during it. As part of your preparation, ask yourself how and why the other negotiator might resist your ask and be ready to respond with additional information. Doing so will help you identify and prepare for the setbacks and challenges that could stand in the way of agreement. The more you prepare, the less anxious you will feel.

During the negotiation, self-distancing is a helpful tool for managing in-the-moment emotions like anger, anxiety, or frustration. Because emotions like anxiety and anger come up when our core identities are threatened, they are easier to manage when we understand our triggers.[10] Pause a negotiation and step back from the trigger event when you sense these feelings coming on.[11] Take some space to reflect on the underlying reasons for your emotions and formulate a strategy to address them. Keeping an emotion diary to document the events that set off your feelings or discussing them with a trusted colleague can help.[12] Over time, you will be able to identity your triggers and act preemptively to manage them.

After the negotiation, try to avoid carrying negative emotions. Focus instead on how you will leverage your experience to be more effective next time.[13] Record the positive capabilities and strengths that you have displayed in the face of challenges, and reflect on the moments you were most proud of during your interaction. The goal of this exercise is to identify how you benefited from the experience and how you can use your strengths to get the result you want in the future.

Challenge #3: Overcoming Interpersonal Resistance

Power plays, like questioning competence or dismissing ideas, are often used to influence or undermine others.[14] These moves create resistance, making it more difficult for individuals to advance their goals in a negotiation.

During our interviews, women gave examples of resistance such as a manager missing a scheduled negotiation, showing horror and surprise at an ask, or being volatile and unpredictable in order to create uncertainty and pessimism. Such interactions were seen as aggressive and intended to derail or stall negotiations, putting women on the back foot and discouraging them from effectively stating their needs.

We know that women face more resistance in negotiations than men, and building capacity to persist despite it emerged as a clear theme in our interviews.[15] Many women stressed the importance of "regrouping and trying again" rather than viewing obstacles as failures.

How can you overcome the challenge?

Building grit is key. Research shows that successful people spend up to one and a half years negotiating and galvanizing support to reshape organizational policies and structures to meet their needs.[16] This means that women will be more successful if they have the confidence to overcome obstacles and persist in the face of resistance. The ability to display flexibility and creativity is a critical first step. Stop framing setbacks as "showstoppers" that close the conversation and start framing them as opportunities to learn more about your counterparts. Ask "why" or "why not" more often. Every setback gives you knowledge about the forms of resistance you can expect in the future and from whom. Use this information to develop a repertoire of constructive responses to resistance.[17]

We identified two broad themes from our interviews. The first theme addressed women's need to boost their confidence by strengthening their core negotiation skills. The second theme, which we focused on, addressed challenges unique to women. These challenges acknowledge that women and men experience negotiations differently. They also show just how much gender stereotypes underpin women's experiences, in how they both perceive negotiations and are perceived as negotiators. Remember, though, they are not insurmountable. You can come to the table resistance-ready, better able to manage your emotions, and actually get what you want.

Adapted from "3 of the Most Common Challenges Women Face in Negotiations," on hbr.org, September 30, 2019 (product #H056DA).

5

Look and Sound Confident During Any Presentation

by Carmine Gallo

You've crafted the message and created the slides. Now it's time to wow the audience with your presentation. How you look and sound are going to make a big impression—and your audience will form opinions quickly.[1]

Research shows that people form impressions about a leader's presentation competence in as little as half a minute.[2] This means, within seconds, listeners will decide whether you are trustworthy, and they will do it based on your body language and vocal attributes. What you say *and* how you say it are equally important.

The good news is that there is plenty of hard evidence that explains how you can give the appearance of confidence and competence—even if you're nervous or timid on the inside.

How to Look Confident

Make eye contact

Making eye contact is the first step to building trust with your listeners. "Eyes play a key role in human social encounters," according to one research report.[3] "When humans observe others' faces, eyes are typically the first features that are scanned for information."

There's a simple way to get better at this, but it takes a little work: Record yourself practicing your presentation or pitch in front of a small audience. Watch the recording, noting all of the times you look at your slides or your notes instead of at your audience. Practice, and record again. Every time you do, try to spend less time talking to the slides and more time making eye contact with your listeners. Rehearse until you have what you want to say down cold.

Keep an open posture

Open posture means that there's no barrier between you and the audience. This includes your arms. An uncomfortable speaker might unconsciously cross their arms, forming a defensive pose without being aware that they're doing it. Confident speakers, by contrast, keep their arms uncrossed with their palms turned up.

But your hands and arms are just one barrier. There are others to eliminate. A laptop between you and your listener is a barrier. Set it to the side. If you keep your hands in your pockets, take them out. An open posture takes up more space and makes you feel more confident. If you feel confident, you'll look confident.

Use gestures

Confident speakers use gestures to reinforce their key points. One study found that entrepreneurs pitching investors were more persuasive when they used a combination of figurative language (stories, metaphors) and gestures to emphasize their message.[4]

Find areas of your presentation where gestures will come across as natural and use them to highlight key points or emphasize a concept. If you're listing a number of items, use your fingers to count them off. If you're talking about something that's wide or expansive, stretch your arms and hands apart. One analysis of popular TED speakers, like Brené Brown and Tony Robbins, found that they tend to bring their hands to their heart when sharing personal stories.[5] Your gestures will reflect your feeling toward the topic you're discussing and invite your listeners to engage with you on a deeper, emotional level.

How to Sound Confident

Eliminate filler words

Avoid words that serve no purpose except to fill the space between sentences. These are words like *um, ah, like,* and the dreaded, *you know?*[6] Excessive filler words can be irritating to listeners and make speakers sound unsure of themselves. Eliminating them is also one of the simplest habits to fix.

Start by studying the verbal delivery of sports commentators. The ones who are at the top of their game rarely use filler words. Instead, before speaking, they think about what they want to communicate next and deliver their comments precisely and concisely.

How did they get there? By spending hours reviewing videos of their performances.

Use this same strategy. Record yourself presenting. Play it back. Your goal is to gain awareness around the filler words you use most. Write them down and practice again. When you catch yourself about to use one, err on silence instead to develop a smoother, polished delivery.

Take time to pause

Most people use filler words because they're afraid of silence. It takes confidence to use dramatic pauses. A pause is like the period in a written sentence. It gives your listener a break between thoughts.

A simple way to learn the power of the pause is to choose one or two phrases in your next presentation that express the key message you want to leave your audience with. Pause before you deliver those lines. For example, "The most important thing I'd like you to remember is this . . . " Pause for two beats before you complete the sentence. Whatever you say next will be instantly memorable.

Vary your pace

Confident speakers vary the pace of their verbal delivery. They slow down and speed up to accentuate their most important points.

Audiobooks are recorded at a moderate pace of 150 to 160 words per minute.[7] It's slow enough to be understood, but not so fast that the listener has a hard time keeping up. TED speakers, similarly, speak around 163 words per minute, right in the sweet spot.

But here's the trick. The best speakers speed up to around 220 words a minute when they want to embellish a certain story detail and keep listeners engaged.[8] When they want to accentuate a certain message, they pause, then deliver their words at a slower pace.

Take TED speaker and human rights attorney Bryan Stevenson. He is a masterful speaker, constantly varying his pace to keep the audience riveted. In one anecdote about meeting civil rights hero Rosa Parks, Stevenson sped up when he rattled off a long list of what his nonprofit intended to accomplish.

I began giving her my rap. I said, "Well, we're trying to challenge injustice. We're trying to help people who have been wrongly convicted. We're trying to confront bias and discrimination in the administration of criminal justice. We're trying to end life without parole sentences for children. We're trying to do something about the death penalty. We're trying to reduce the prison population. We're trying to end mass incarceration."

Stevenson then dramatically slowed down the pace of his speech to deliver Park's response: "She looked at me and she said, 'Mmm mmm mmm. That's going to make you tired, tired, tired.'"

The audience laughed, touched by the story. Stevenson's varied and controlled delivery made a story that could have been dry and predictable, poignant, and humorous. He never leaves his delivery to chance.

How can you master this skill? Let the story you are trying to tell guide you. Don't force it, but if there's a part in your presentation where it makes sense to rattle off a series of words or sentences—perhaps a section in which you need to run through a list of details—try speeding it up. Then, slow it down as you approach your main point.

It's the rare presenter who's mastered all six of these principles of confident speaking. Practice, practice, practice. Don't be hard on yourself if it takes more time than you expect. Some of these tactics will take a couple of runthroughs to get right, while others—like pacing—require hours of work and advanced delivery skills to nail down. Keep at it. There is nothing more influential than the power of your presence matching the power of your ideas.

Adapted from "How to Look and Sound Confident During a Presentation," on hbr.org, October 23, 2019 (product #H058ID).

6

How to Negotiate—
Virtually

by Hal Movius

A n increasing number of dealmakers were connecting through digital tools even before the Covid-19 pandemic. Video technologies, low-cost teleconferencing, and digital collaboration platforms have all become efficient ways for teams to prepare together and to negotiate with counterparts.

What does research tell us about virtual negotiations? Are they more or less effective at creating value for counterparties?

The picture is mixed.

First, the bad news: Negotiating virtually tends to leave parties with poorer objective results and feeling less warmth and trust toward one another.[1] Moreover, a meta-analysis conducted in 2002 suggests that group decision-making is less effective, less satisfying, and more protracted when groups don't communicate face-to-face.[2]

When it comes to email—which introverts are particularly drawn to in conflict situations—we tend to be less cooperative, perhaps because we are less inhibited in expressing complaints and negative opinions.[3] We also run a greater risk of misunderstandings: Justin Kruger, Nick Epley, and their colleagues have found that we tend to overestimate how well recipients have understood our messages.[4] And another study suggests that—surprise, surprise—we're also worse at reading emotions over email.[5]

Interestingly, a meta-analysis of 43 studies suggests that women are less cooperative in virtual settings than they are when face-to-face, whereas men's tactics don't change as much. It may be that women feel less pressure to be affiliative or polite when they are not face-to-face.[6]

If virtual negotiators face additional barriers to finding joint gains, the good news is that research also suggests ways to increase your success in virtual settings.

Planning Virtual Negotiations

Preparation is the key to success in any negotiation, and a virtual setting is no different in that respect.

- **Assign clear roles to your team.** Calls or videoconferences with four or more parties can quickly go off track. Ask: Who will open the meeting? Explain a proposal? Answer questions? Summarize next steps? How will we communicate with one another?

- **Specify—and practice with—off-line methods for chatting.** There are many cringe-worthy stories of "private" messages accidentally appearing on everyone's screen. To avoid this, use different hardware or programs for chatting. If you're using a computer to videoconference, for example, use your phone and a separate application to chat or text with teammates.

- **Keep chatting brief.** Messaging during negotiations can be important, but one study found that multitasking on a smartphone while negotiating led to lower payoffs and being rated as less professional and less trustworthy by counterparts.[7] When communicating with teammates during a negotiation, brevity is a virtue.

- **Use video—the bigger, the better.** Charles Naquin and his colleagues found that negotiators communicating by video performed better than negotiators using email or texting.[8] And those using a large computer screen performed better than those using a small one. The easier it is to see your counterparts, the less effort your brain will waste.

- **Keep it short and sweet.** While video and tele-
phone conferencing are "richer" media than email
or text, they are also more cognitively taxing.
Human brains are prediction machines, and they
must work extra hard to understand gaps, glitches,
time lags, and other ambiguities in the interaction.
Short, structured video- and teleconferences can
help keep parties engaged and at their best.

Leading Virtual Negotiations

Conducting a virtual negotiation builds on the best
practices of traditional, around-the-table meetings.

- **Connect at the outset.** Taking a few minutes to
schmooze or make small talk at the start of a meeting can help set the stage for a more collaborative
interaction. Research by Michael Morris and his
colleagues found that when emailing, subjects who
were randomly assigned to make small talk for a
few minutes before negotiating achieved better financial and social outcomes than those who began
negotiating immediately.[9] In another experiment,
starting a negotiation with humor led to better economic outcomes and better feelings between parties.[10] Particularly in stressful situations, making a
personal connection can have a powerful effect on
what follows.

- **Clarify constraints and assumptions.** Video meetings and teleconferences can often have "ragged" starts where parties join at different times and sort out technical glitches. After taking time to connect, quickly clarify the meeting purpose and the time to be committed. If a key party will have to leave early, for example, reshape the agenda as needed at the outset.

- **Hide your self-view.** For Americans and others from more individualized Western cultures, evidence suggests that seeing yourself during a video call tends to increase self-consciousness and self-criticism.[11] Particularly if you already have these tendencies, consider turning off the self-view when videoconferencing.

There's no substitute for the richness of negotiating in a face-to-face environment. But digital communication tools and media can make negotiations more efficient and can help us to stay connected—provided that we understand how to put them to best use.

Adapted from content posted on hbr.org, June 10, 2020 (product #H05OO0).

7

The Most Overused Negotiating Tactic Is Threatening to Walk Away

by Jay A. Hewlin

Professional negotiators and researchers alike hail the BATNA (best alternative to a negotiated agreement, or "walk away" outcome) as a negotiator's primary source of relative power.[1] But relying on even the best of alternatives as leverage can be tricky business.

Your relative power in a negotiation is your capacity to *use resources to influence another's circumstances*, and a BATNA's role in that regard can range anywhere from significant to nonexistent. Consider the obvious challenge of a negotiator who thinks she has a very strong alternative but discovers that the other side has a relatively stronger one. This type of BATNA asymmetry can occur in several varieties (for example, no BATNA versus strong BATNA, or deals where the incentives on each side are completely different). A negotiator's BATNA-based power in these situations is virtually meaningless, as would be any corresponding strategy based on the same.

BATNAs help negotiators establish minimum or maximum thresholds beyond which a deal with a particular negotiator is of no value. In essence, they are a defense against an inferior agreement. They are *not* designed to facilitate relationship building, exploration, creativity, or collaboration, all of which most researchers and practitioners agree are necessary to reach the often sought for, but rarely achieved, optimal or "efficient" agreement.[2] Negotiators can take practical steps toward a more constructive approach to maximize the integrative potential of their negotiations.

Think Mutual Dependence, Not Just Alternatives

Ascertaining why and how deeply one's counterparty needs what you're offering is central when it comes to relative power—the greater their need for you or your product or service, the greater your power, and vice versa. So spend your efforts focusing on the power inherent in your mutual dependence.[3] Mutual dependence is determined by the sum or the average of Party A's dependence on Party B, and Party B's dependence on Party A. The connection between mutual dependence and power is direct, and it exists in *every* negotiation.

Focusing on mutual dependence draws your attention toward inquiry and exploration, advancing the conversation from: "How much can I get out of this deal above my best alternative?" to "In how many ways can I demonstrate my company's value to this person based on their need(s)?"

This is precisely how entrepreneur John Settles, co-owner of a relatively new company specializing in sustainability, pitched his company to a local school district. John had no previous relationship with the buyer, his business was new, and his track record was limited. His competition comprised larger and more established corporations, and alternatives, as such, were irrelevant. John rightly focused on asking probing questions and not only was able to identify how his company was uniquely positioned to serve the immediate needs of the district, but also designed a multitiered plan that deepened the buyer's interest and need for his company's services. John turned the conversation toward ways they could mutually benefit in those areas where their mutual needs overlapped. Together, the two created a better deal—one that could potentially yield 25% more than the one they initially met to discuss.

Find Power in Your Context, Not Your Feelings

You'll often hear the following statement: *"When I feel I have more power in a negotiation, I negotiate better, but when the situation is reversed, I don't do as well."* Limited research has been done on the issue of negotiators' perceptions of power and how those perceptions affect outcomes, providing some evidence of a positive relationship between negotiators' perceptions of their power and the degree to which they engage in integrative bargaining.[4]

The challenge with power that fluctuates with feelings is that this type of power often results in negotiators seeking to capture value, using their power to behave more opportunistically, and leaving the other side feeling as though their interests are not being considered.[5] On the other hand, the "feelings analyses" can leave negotiators feeling insecure and not being assertive enough. Power in a negotiation is *not* based on your subjective and limited view of what you have to offer, but rather on the objective reality of what you have to offer in relation to the need of the other party. Feelings of power are irrelevant.

Focusing on mutual dependence can again be helpful here, providing greater psychological power for situations where positional power (or role power) and BATNA power are absent.[6] For example, several undergraduate and graduate students have shared stories of their challenging hiring and promotion negotiations where these students had a weak or no BATNA and felt that the employer was in the stronger position. By focusing on the power present in the respective needs of the companies in relation to their skills, they didn't feel powerless. They strategically framed the narrative around the value of mutual gain that could be achieved by hiring or promoting them. Outcomes included 10%–30% increases in their incoming salary offers, higher bonuses, better titles, and more vacation time. Moreover, hiring managers frequently applauded these candidates for being assertive. They felt more confident hiring someone who could respectfully, artfully, and convincingly fight for what they felt they deserved.

Focus on Learning, Not Buying or Selling

Three priorities during a negotiation should be:

- Learning as much as possible about the person with whom you are dealing

- Learning as much as possible about the entity with which you are dealing

- Ascertaining as much as possible about their circumstances

Who is this person? How many years have they been working in this industry? How long have they been working for this organization? How is this person rewarded in their organization? Is this a big project for this person or entity, or a small, relatively insignificant project? How many such projects are they handling currently?

Related questions would be: What kind of organization is this? How long has it been in business? How does it define its market, or in the case of a nongovernmental or government agency, its central purpose? What is its current place in that market, and what does it want its strategic place to be in the market in the near future and longer term?

Structure your early questions as generalities. You don't want to come across too aggressively, especially with negotiators who are less inclined to answer too many questions. As the negotiation proceeds, you can transition to more specific questions. You know the other party needs your product or service, but why? How can you satisfy this party's need and make them more financially or otherwise dependent on you or your product?

Treat the Unknown as a Place of Hidden Potential, Not a Frightening Minefield

Negotiations are won mostly at the preparation table, not the negotiation table. Research the market, the person, the entity, and so on, but don't feel bound by the limitations of that information. The facts that you have indicate only some, but certainly not all, of the probabilities.

The most emotionally challenging aspect of preparation involves embracing the unknown as a place of potential in the negotiation. The critical question is: "What don't I know that I need to know?" While information asymmetry can be the most unsettling aspect of negotiating, it can also be the most interesting. This is because the discovery of information on both sides of the table provides opportunities for creative solutions. When fear causes a negotiator to hide information, that negotiator (and perhaps their counterpart) works against the formation of a deal, not for it. So, don't spend all of your preparation time determining how to *lock* in a deal. Instead, spend time brainstorming and identifying questions that, once answered, will help you *unlock* ideas.

Negotiation by its very nature requires compromise, which means there is no such thing as absolute power in negotiations. Every negotiator has some power, and there's always some degree of mutual dependence. So don't short-circuit your main power source because you're so focused on alternative power sources. Your BATNA can help you determine what is probable if the current deal fails to materialize; however, it's incapable of revealing a deal's full potential. Only you and your counterpart working together at the table have the power to create a deal that not only exceeds the BATNA but perhaps makes it altogether irrelevant.

Adapted from content posted on hbr.org, September 18, 2017 (product #H03WA1).

8

How to Bounce Back After a Failed Negotiation

by Carolyn O'Hara

Sometimes, despite your best efforts, a negotiation doesn't go your way. Perhaps a customer pushed for a steeper discount than you wanted to give, or a potential client went with a competitor's approach to a project. In the face of a disappointment—one where you might appear to be the "loser"—how do you save face? How do you make sure your reputation isn't damaged and the relationship with your counterpart is intact?

What the Experts Say

Don't worry too much about your negotiating prowess just because you lost this round. "A reputation comes from consistent behavior," says Jeff Weiss, founding partner at Vantage Partners, a Boston-based consultancy specializing in corporate negotiations, and author of the *HBR Guide to Negotiating*. If you learn from the experience, there's value to be had. A good way to start is by abandoning the adversarial mindset. "If all you're thinking about is saving face, you've already made the negotiation and its aftermath into a battle," says Margaret Neale, the Adams Distinguished Professor of Management at Stanford Graduate School of Business and coauthor of *Getting (More of) What You Want*. Think instead in terms of solutions so that your approach "becomes about problem solving rather than someone trying to win." That's where real win-win scenarios begin to emerge. Here's how to bounce back when a negotiation doesn't go your way.

Don't panic

Take a deep breath and think about how to contain your losses. "Don't assume that this is the end of the world," says Weiss. More often than not "this is one transaction of many," and there will be opportunities in the future to retry your case. You might also be overestimating the degree to which this outcome has dented your business position or reputation. Sure, you may not have gotten the price you wanted, for example, but that doesn't necessarily mean the customer thinks you're a pushover. "Don't assume you lost face," Neale says. "It's like that old saying:

You wouldn't care so much about what other people think if you knew how little they think about you."

Look for a bright side

You may not have "won" on the terms you came to the table with, but there may be some unexplored upside that you haven't yet considered. "You're never going to get 100% of what you want," says Neale. But the best negotiators will find value and benefits in unexpected places. Perhaps you aren't getting as big an order as you'd like, but you've cemented a valuable client relationship going forward. "Ask yourself if you can tie some other detail to a piece of the deal," suggests Weiss. "Are there other terms and conditions where you can balance this out in some way or make some sort of a trade?" That doesn't mean frantically trying to renegotiate unfavorable terms, which could make you appear desperate. But it does mean thinking about how, for example, the lower profits you're accepting might be balanced out by opening up new markets.

Be up-front about your missteps

So you didn't land the big client. Don't sequester yourself out of frustration. Doing so is unhelpful and prevents you from controlling the narrative with your employees and managers. "Consider whether there are people internally you need to talk to, to get out ahead of this," says Weiss. "Ask yourself whether there is anything you need to convey to your colleagues about why this happened and what it means." Neale agrees, adding that being open about missteps is particularly important for executives, who often serve as role models. "Both learning from your mistakes and admitting to those mistakes are important for being a better leader," she says. If you're transparent, then your employees are more likely to do the same when a negotiation doesn't go their way.

Leverage the future

Don't think about this disappointment as the end of the story. "When you don't get the outcome you want," says Neale, "set up for the next negotiation." While you're still at the table, position yourself for the next deal. "You might frame it as a game of favors and ledgers," says Weiss. For example, you might stress that the client has gotten a good deal from you because you've worked together for so long and you value their business. Or that because they've helped you solve problems in the past, you're helping them solve a problem now. Try to focus the conversation on the road ahead. "You might say, 'This one is a bit lopsided, but we can start thinking now about the next negotiation,'" says Weiss. That way you're expanding this particular negotiation into a series of conversations.

Do a postmortem

Take the time to reflect on why you ended up on the disappointing end of the deal in the first place. "Ask yourself, 'How did I get here? How did they put me in a corner?'" says Weiss. Perhaps you didn't fully understand what your counterpart's interests were or you didn't adequately prepare for a pivot at the table. Think about your negotiating process: Was your messaging or positioning incorrect? Though you may not have done as well as you'd like, tomorrow is another day. "Stay focused on the long term," says Neale. "This is just one of many battles."

Case Study: Look for Unexpected Benefits

Samantha Spector, founder of Saloonbox, a monthly subscription cocktail kit, was finding it hard to hide her disappointment. Her startup had begun holding meetings for outside financing, and a major potential investor wanted her to lower the company's valuation—by 60%. "We were surprised," Spector said. "They said our value was way off. If we had gone into the conversation knowing that, we might have thought, 'Oh no, maybe we don't want to talk to them.'"

Spector thought about getting angry and walking away. "But instead of ending the conversation," she says, "we decided to explore what exactly they could do [if they invested in us]."

The investor had a great deal of operational experience and could offer consulting, assistance with the company's pricing structure, and introductions for relationships that would be helpful. Ultimately, Spector decided to keep the negotiations open because of the benefits the investor brought to the table.

"It showed us that it's really important to listen, ask a lot of questions, and not go into a negotiation with a firm idea of something," she says. "Even if you think, 'I want to storm away,' it's always in your best interests to hear somebody out."

After the initial disappointing conversation, Spector says, "We really realized that we could make a lot more in the long run from this kind of partnership if we were willing to give up a little bit more in the beginning."

Adapted from content posted on hbr.org, April 21, 2016 (product #H02U09).

Manage Your Emotions

9

Emotion and the Art of Negotiation

by Alison Wood Brooks

t is, without question, my favorite day of the semester—
the day when I teach my MBA students a negotiation
exercise called "Honoring the Contract."

I assign students to partners, and each reads a different
account of a (fictitious) troubled relationship between a
supplier (a manufacturer of computer components) and
a client (a search engine startup). They learn that the two
parties signed a detailed contract eight months earlier,
but now they're at odds over several of the terms (sales
volume, pricing, product reliability, and energy efficiency
specs). Each student assumes the role of either client or
supplier and receives confidential information about company finances and politics. Then each pair is tasked with
renegotiating—a process that could lead to an amended
deal, termination of the contract, or expensive litigation.

What makes this simulation interesting, however, lies not in the details of the case but in the top-secret instructions given to one side of each pairing before the exercise begins: "Please start the negotiation with a display of anger. You must display anger for a minimum of 10 minutes at the beginning." The instructions go on to give specific tips for showing anger: Interrupt the other party. Call her "unfair" or "unreasonable." Blame her personally for the disagreement. Raise your voice.

Before the negotiations begin, I spread the pairs all over the building so that the students can't see how others are behaving. Then, as the pairs negotiate, I walk around and observe. Although some students struggle, many are spectacularly good at feigning anger. They wag a finger in their partner's face. They pace around. I've never seen the exercise result in a physical confrontation—but it has come close. Some of the negotiators who did not get the secret instructions react by trying to defuse the other person's anger. But some react angrily themselves—and it's amazing how quickly the emotional responses escalate. When I bring everyone back into the classroom after 30 minutes, there are always students still yelling at each other or shaking their heads in disbelief.

During the debriefing, we survey the pairs to see how angry they felt and how they fared in resolving the problem. Often, the more anger the parties showed, the more likely it was that the negotiation ended poorly—for example, in litigation or an impasse (no deal). Once I've clued the entire class in on the setup, discussion invariably makes its way to this key insight: Bringing anger to a negotiation is like throwing a bomb into the process, and it's apt to have a profound effect on the outcome.

Until 20 years ago, few researchers paid much attention to the role of emotions in negotiating—how feelings can influence the way people overcome conflict, reach agreement, and create value when dealing with another party. Instead, negotiation scholars focused primarily on strategy and tactics—particularly the ways in which parties can identify and consider alternatives, use leverage, and execute the choreography of offers and counteroffers. Scientific understanding of negotiation also tended to home in on the transactional nature of working out a deal: how to get the most money or profit from the process. Even when experts started looking at psychological influences on negotiations, they focused on diffuse and nonspecific moods—such as whether negotiators felt generally positive or negative, and how that affected their behavior.

Over the past decade, however, researchers have begun examining how specific emotions—anger, sadness, disappointment, anxiety, envy, excitement, and regret—can affect the behavior of negotiators. They've studied the differences between what happens when people simply feel these emotions and what happens when they also express them to the other party through words or actions. In negotiations that are less transactional and involve parties in long-term relationships, understanding the role of emotions is even more important than it is in transactional dealmaking.

This new branch of research is proving extremely useful. We all have the ability to regulate how we experience emotions, and specific strategies can help us improve tremendously in that regard. We also have some control over the extent to which we express our feelings—and again, there are specific ways to cloak (or emphasize) an expression of emotion when doing so may be advantageous. For instance, research shows that feeling or looking anxious results in suboptimal negotiation outcomes. So individuals who are prone to anxiety when brokering a deal can take certain steps both to limit their nervousness and to make it less obvious to their negotiation opponent. The same is true for other emotions.

In the pages that follow, I discuss—and share coping strategies for—many of the emotions people typically feel over the course of a negotiation (see table 9-1). Anxiety is most likely to crop up before the process begins or during its early stages. We're prone to experience anger or excitement in the heat of the discussions. And we're most likely to feel disappointment, sadness, or regret in the aftermath.

TABLE 9-1

Preparing your emotional strategy

Preparation is key to success in negotiations. It's vital to give advance thought to the objective factors involved (Who are the parties? What are the issues? What is my best outside option if we don't reach a deal?), but it is perhaps even more important to prepare your emotional strategy. Use the following questions and tips to plan ahead for each stage of the negotiation.

	Ask yourself	Remember
The buildup	• How do I feel? • Should I express my emotions? • How might the people across the table feel? • Are they likely to hide or express their emotions? • Should I recruit a third party to negotiate on my behalf?	• It's normal to feel anxious and excited. • Try to avoid expressing anxiety. • Expressing forward-looking excitement may help build rapport. • In emotionally charged situations (such as a divorce), consider having a third party (such as a lawyer) negotiate on your behalf.
The main event	• What things could happen that would make me feel angry? • What things might I do that would trigger my counterparts to feel angry? • What might they do or ask that would make me feel anxious?	• Be careful about expressing anger; it may extract concessions but harm the long-term relationship. • Avoid angering your counterparts; they are likely to walk away. • Preparing answers to tough questions is critical for staying calm in the moment.
The finale	• What are the possible outcomes of the negotiation? What do I hope to achieve? What do I expect to achieve? • How would those outcomes make me feel? • Should I express those feelings? To whom? • How are my counterparts likely to feel about the possible outcomes?	• To reduce disappointment, outline clear aspirations and expectations and adjust them throughout the negotiation. • When you feel pleased about an outcome, it may be wise to keep it to yourself. • The best negotiators create value for everyone, claiming the lion's share for themselves but making their counterparts feel that they, too, won.

Avoiding Anxiety

Anxiety is a state of distress in reaction to threatening stimuli, particularly novel situations that have the potential for undesirable outcomes. In contrast to anger, which motivates people to escalate conflict (the "fight" part of the fight-or-flight response), anxiety trips the "flight" switch and makes people want to exit the scene.

Because patience and persistence are often desirable when negotiating, the urge to exit quickly is counterproductive. But the negative effects of feeling anxious while negotiating may go further. In my recent research, I wondered if anxious negotiators also develop low aspirations and expectations, which could lead them to make timid first offers—a behavior that directly predicts poor negotiating outcomes.

In work with Maurice Schweitzer in 2011, I explored how anxiety influences negotiations. First we surveyed 185 professionals about the emotions they expected to feel before negotiating with a stranger, negotiating to buy a car, and negotiating to increase their salary. When dealing with a stranger or asking for a higher salary, anxiety was the dominant emotional expectation; when negotiating for the car, anxiety was second only to excitement.

To understand how anxiety can affect negotiators, we then asked a separate group of 136 participants to negotiate a cell phone contract that required agreeing on a purchase price, a warranty period, and the length of the contract. We induced anxiety in half the participants by having them listen to continuous three-minute clips of the menacing theme music from the film *Psycho*, while the other half listened to pleasant music by Handel. (Researchers call this "incidental" emotional manipulation, and it's quite powerful. Listening to the *Psycho* music is genuinely uncomfortable: People's palms get sweaty, and some listeners become jumpy.)

In this experiment and three others, we found that anxiety had a significant effect on how people negotiated. People experiencing anxiety made weaker first offers, responded more quickly to each move the counterpart made, and were more likely to exit negotiations early (even though their instructions clearly warned that exiting early would reduce the value they received from the negotiation). Anxious negotiators made deals that were 12% less financially attractive than those made by negotiators in the neutral group. We did discover one caveat, however: People who gave themselves high ratings in a survey on negotiating aptitude were less affected by anxiety than others.

Those experiments examined what happens when people feel anxious. But what happens when they express that anxiety, making it clear to their counterparts that they're nervous (and perhaps vulnerable)? In 2012, with Francesca Gino and Maurice Schweitzer, I conducted eight experiments to explore how anxious people behaved in situations in which they could seek advice from others. We found that relative to people who did not feel anxious, they were less confident, more likely to consult others when making decisions, and less able to discriminate between good and bad advice. In the most relevant of these experiments, we found that anxious participants did not discount advice from someone with a stated conflict of interest, whereas subjects feeling neutral emotions looked upon that advice skeptically. Although this research didn't directly address how the subjects would negotiate, it suggests that people who express anxiety are more likely to be taken advantage of in a negotiation, especially if the other party senses their distress.

Excellent negotiators often make their counterparts feel anxious on purpose. For example, on the TV show *Shark Tank*, six wealthy investors (sharks) negotiate with entrepreneurs hoping for funding. The entrepreneurs must pitch their ideas in front of a huge television audience and face questions from the investors that are often aggressive and unnerving. As this is going on, stress-inducing music fills the TV studio. This setup does more than create drama and entertainment for viewers; it also intentionally puts pressure on the entrepreneurs. The sharks are professional negotiators who want to knock the entrepreneurs off balance so that it will be easier to take ownership of their good ideas at the lowest price possible. (When multiple sharks want to invest, they often drop comments that are intended to make opposing investors anxious too.) If you watch the show closely, you'll probably notice a pattern: The entrepreneurs who seem least rattled by the environmental stressors tend to negotiate the most carefully and deliberately—and often strike the best deals.

The takeaway from both research and practice is clear: Try your utmost to avoid feeling anxious while negotiating. How can you manage that? Train, practice, rehearse, and keep sharpening your negotiating skills. Anxiety is often a response to novel stimuli, so the more familiar the stimuli, the more comfortable and the less anxious you will feel. (That's why clinicians who treat anxiety disorders often rely on exposure therapy: People who are nervous about flying on airplanes, for instance, are progressively exposed to the experience, first getting used to the sights and sounds, then sitting in airliner seats, and ultimately taking flights.) Indeed, although many people enroll in negotiation classes to learn strategies and increase skills, one of the primary benefits is the comfort that comes from repeatedly practicing dealmaking in simulations and exercises. Negotiation eventually feels more routine, so it's not such an anxiety-inducing experience.

Another useful strategy for reducing anxiety is to bring in an outside expert to handle the bargaining. Third-party negotiators will be less anxious because their skills are better honed, the process is routine for them, and they have a lower personal stake in the outcome. Outsourcing your negotiation may sound like a cop-out, but it's a frequent practice in many industries. Home buyers and sellers use real estate brokers partly for their negotiating experience; athletes, authors, actors, and even some business executives rely on agents to hammer out contracts. Although there are costs to this approach, they are often more than offset by the more favorable terms that can be achieved. And although anxious negotiators may have the most to gain from involving a third party (because anxiety can be a particularly difficult emotion to regulate in an uncomfortable setting), this strategy can also be useful when other negative emotions surface.

Managing Anger

Like anxiety, anger is a negative emotion, but instead of being self-focused, it's usually directed toward someone else. In most circumstances, we try to keep our tempers in check. When it comes to negotiating, however, many people believe that anger can be a productive emotion—one that will help them win a larger share of the pie.

This view stems from a tendency to view negotiations in competitive terms rather than collaborative ones. Researchers call this the fixed-pie bias: People, particularly those with limited experience making deals, assume that a negotiation is a zero-sum game in which their own interests conflict directly with a counterpart's. (More-experienced negotiators, in contrast, look for ways to expand the pie through collaboration, rather than nakedly trying to snatch a bigger slice.) Anger, the thinking goes, makes one seem stronger, more powerful, and better able to succeed in this grab for value.

In fact, there's a body of research—much of it by Keith Allred, a former faculty member at Harvard's Kennedy School of Government—that documents the consequences of feeling angry while negotiating. This research shows that anger often harms the process by escalating conflict, biasing perceptions, and making impasses more likely. It also reduces joint gains, decreases cooperation, intensifies competitive behavior, and increases the rate at which offers are rejected. Angry negotiators are less accurate than neutral negotiators both in recalling their own interests and in judging other parties' interests. And angry negotiators may seek to harm or retaliate against their counterparts, even though a more cooperative approach might increase the value that both sides can claim from the negotiation.

Despite these findings, many people continue to see advantages to feeling or appearing angry. Some even attempt to turn up the volume on their anger, because they think it will make them more effective in a negotiation. In my own research, I have found that given a choice between feeling angry and feeling happy while negotiating, more than half the participants want to be in an angry state and view it as significantly advantageous.

There *are* cases when feeling angry can lead to better outcomes. Research by Gerben van Kleef at the University of Amsterdam demonstrates that in a onetime transactional negotiation with few opportunities to collaborate to create value, an angry negotiator can wind up with a better deal. There may even be situations in which a negotiator decides to feign anger, because the counterpart, in an attempt to defuse that anger, is likely to give ground on terms. This might work well if you are haggling with a stranger to buy a car, for example.

But negotiators who play this card must be aware of the costs. Showing anger in a negotiation damages the long-term relationship between the parties. It reduces liking and trust. Research by Rachel Campagna at the University of New Hampshire shows that false representations of anger may generate small tactical benefits but also lead to considerable and persistent blowback. That is, faking anger can create authentic feelings of anger, which in turn diminish trust for both parties. Along the same lines, research by Jeremy Yip and Martin Schweinsberg demonstrates that people who encounter an angry negotiator are more likely to walk away, preferring to let the process end in a stalemate.

In many contexts, then, feeling or expressing anger as a negotiating tactic can backfire. So in most cases, tamping down any anger you feel—and limiting the anger you express—is a smarter strategy. This may be hard to do, but there are tactics that can help.

Building rapport before, during, and after a negotiation can reduce the odds that the other party will become angry. If you seek to frame the negotiation cooperatively—to make it clear that you're seeking a win-win solution instead of trying to get the lion's share of a fixed pie—you may limit the other party's perception that an angry grab for value will work well. If the other party does become angry, apologize. Seek to soothe. Even if you feel that his anger is unwarranted, recognize that you're almost certainly better positioned tactically if you can reduce the hostility. (For more, see the sidebar "Managing Your Counterpart's Emotions.")

Perhaps the most effective way to deal with anger in negotiations is to recognize that many negotiations don't unfold all at once but take place over multiple meetings. So if tensions are flaring, ask for a break, cool off, and regroup. This isn't easy when you're angry, because your fight-or-flight response urges you to escalate, not pull back. Resist that urge and give the anger time to dissipate. In heated negotiations, hitting the pause button can be the smartest play.

Finally, you might consider reframing anger as sadness. Though reframing one negative emotion as another sounds illogical, shared feelings of sadness can lead to cooperative concession making, whereas oppositional anger often leads to an impasse.

Managing Your Counterpart's Emotions

Negotiating is an interpersonal process. There will always be at least one other party (and often many more) involved. In the adjoining article I discuss how to manage your own emotions during a negotiation. But what about the other people at the table? Can you manage their emotions as well? I suggest two strategies for doing so.

- **Be observant.** Perceiving how other people are feeling is a critical component of emotional intelligence, and it's particularly key in negotiations (as Adam Galinsky and his colleagues have found). So tune in to your counterpart's body language, tone of voice, and choice of words. When her verbal and nonverbal cues don't match up, ask questions. For example, "You are telling me you like this outcome, but you seem uneasy. Is something making you uncomfortable?" Or "You say you're angry, but you seem somewhat pleased. Are you truly upset about something? Or are you trying to intimidate me?"

  Asking pointed questions based on your perceptions of the other party's emotional expressions will make it easier for you to understand her perspective (a task people are shockingly bad at, according to research by Nicholas Epley). It will also make it difficult for a counterpart to lie to you; evidence suggests that people prefer to tell lies of omission about facts rather than lies of commission about feelings.

- **Don't be afraid to exert direct influence on your counterpart's emotions.** This may sound manipulative or even unscrupulous, but you can use this influence for good. For example, if your counterpart seems anxious or angry, injecting humor or empathetic reassurance can dramatically change the tone of the interaction. By the same token, if your counterpart seems overconfident or pushy, expressing well-placed anger can inspire a healthy dose of fear.

In recent research with Elizabeth Baily Wolf, I have found that it's possible to go even further in managing others' emotions: You display an emotion, your counterpart sees it, and then you shape his interpretation of it. For example, imagine that you start crying at work. (Crying is a difficult-to-control and often embarrassing behavior.) Saying "I'm in tears because I'm passionate" rather than "I'm sorry I'm so emotional" can completely change the way others react and the way they view your self-control and competence.

Handling Disappointment and Regret

It can be tempting to see negotiations in binary terms—you either win or lose. Of course, that is generally too simplistic: Most complex negotiations will end with each side having achieved some of its goals and not others—a mix of wins and losses. Still, as a negotiation winds down, it's natural to look at the nascent agreement and feel, on balance, more positive or negative about it.

Disappointment can be a powerful force when it's expressed to the other party near the end of the negotiation. There's a relationship between anger and disappointment—both typically arise when an individual feels wronged—and it's useful to understand how one can be used more constructively than the other. (Think back to how you reacted as a child if your parents said, "I'm very disappointed in you," instead of "I'm very angry with you.") Although expressing anger may create defensiveness or increase the odds of a standoff, expressing disappointment can serve a more tactical purpose by encouraging the other party to look critically at her own actions and consider whether she wants to change her position to reduce the negative feelings she's caused you.

Research shows that one cause of disappointment in a negotiation is the speed of the process. When a negotiation unfolds or concludes too quickly, participants tend to feel dissatisfied. They wonder if they could or should have done more or pushed harder. Negotiation teachers see this in class exercises: Often the first students to finish up are the most disappointed by the outcome. The obvious way to lessen the likelihood of disappointment is to proceed slowly and deliberately.

Regret is slightly different from disappointment. While the latter tends to involve sadness about an outcome, someone feeling regret is looking a little more upstream at the course of actions that led to this unhappy outcome and thinking about the missteps or mistakes that created the disappointment.

Research shows that people are most likely to regret actions they didn't take—the missed opportunities and errors of omission, rather than errors of commission. That can be a powerful insight for negotiators, whose primary actions should be asking questions, listening, proposing solutions, and brainstorming new alternatives if the parties can't agree. Ironically, people often don't ask questions while negotiating: They may forget to raise important matters or feel reluctant to probe too deeply, deeming it invasive or rude. Those fears are often misplaced. In fact, people who ask a lot of questions tend to be better liked, and they learn more things. In negotiations, information is king, and learning should be a central goal. One way to reduce the potential for regret is to ask questions without hesitation. Aim to come away from the negotiation with the sense that every avenue was explored.

Skilled negotiators use another technique to minimize the odds of regret: the "post-settlement settlement." This strategy recognizes that tension often dissipates when there's a deal on the table that makes everyone happy, and sometimes the best negotiating happens after that tension is released. So instead of shaking hands and ending the dealmaking, one party might say, "We're good. We have terms we can all live with. But now that we know we've reached an agreement, let's spend a few more minutes chatting to see if we can find anything that sweetens it for both sides." Done ineptly, this might seem as if one party is trying to renege or renegotiate. However, when handled deftly, a post-settlement settlement can open a pathway for both sides to become even more satisfied with the outcome and stave off regrets.

Tempering Happiness and Excitement

There isn't much research on how happiness and excitement affect negotiations, but intuition and experience suggest that expressing these emotions can have significant consequences. The National Football League prohibits and penalizes "excessive celebrations" after a touchdown or big play because such conduct can generate ill will. For the same reason, the "winner" in a deal should not gloat as the negotiations wrap up. Nonetheless, this happens all the time: In workshops I routinely see students unabashedly boast and brag (sometimes to the entire class) about how they really stuck it to their opponents in a negotiation exercise. Not only do these students risk looking like jerks, but in a real-world setting they might suffer more-dire consequences, such as the other party's invoking a right of rescission, seeking to renegotiate, or taking punitive action the next time the parties need to strike a deal.

Although it's unpleasant to feel disappointed after a negotiation, it can be even worse to make your counterparts feel that way. And in certain situations, showing happiness or excitement triggers disappointment in others. The best negotiators achieve great deals for themselves but leave their opponents believing that they, too, did fabulously, even if the truth is different. In deals that involve a significant degree of future collaboration—say, when two companies agree to merge, or when an actor signs a contract with a producer to star in an upcoming movie—it can be appropriate to show excitement, but it's important to focus on the opportunities ahead rather than the favorable terms one party just gained.

Another danger of excitement is that it may increase your commitment to strategies or courses of action that you'd be better off abandoning. In my negotiation class, we do an exercise in which students must decide whether or not to send a race car driver into an important race with a faulty engine. Despite the risks, most students opt to go ahead with the race because they are excited and want to maximize their prize winnings. The exercise has parallels to a real-life example: the launch of the *Challenger* space shuttle. Though the engineers who designed the *Challenger*'s faulty O-ring had qualms about it, NASA managers were overly excited and determined to proceed with the launch. Their decision ultimately led to the craft's explosion and the loss of its seven crew members.

There are two lessons for negotiators. First, be considerate: Do not let your excitement make your counterparts feel that they lost. Second, be skeptical: Do not let your excitement lead to overconfidence or an escalation of commitment with insufficient data.

Negotiating requires some of the same skills that playing poker does—a strategic focus, the imagination to see alternatives, and a knack for assessing odds, reading people, understanding others' positions, and bluffing when necessary. However, whereas the parties in a negotiation must strive for agreement, poker players make decisions unilaterally. Poker also lacks win-win outcomes or pie-sharing strategies: Any given hand is generally a zero-sum game, with one player's gains coming directly from the other players' pots.

Nonetheless, negotiators can learn a crucial lesson from the card table: the value of controlling the emotions we feel and especially those we reveal. In other words, good negotiators need to develop a poker face—not one that remains expressionless, always hiding true feelings, but one that displays the right emotions at the right times. And although all human beings experience emotions, the frequency and intensity with which we do so differs from person to person. To be a better dealmaker, conduct a thorough assessment of which emotions you are particularly prone to feel before, during, and after negotiations, and use techniques to minimize (or maximize) the experience and suppress (or emphasize) the expression of emotions as needed.

In one of my favorite scenes from the TV show *30 Rock*, the hard-driving CEO Jack Donaghy (Alec Baldwin), who fancies himself an expert negotiator, explains to a colleague why he struck a poor deal: "I lost because of emotion, which I always thought was a weakness, but now I have learned can also be a weapon." Borrowing Jack's insightful metaphor, I urge you to wield your emotions thoughtfully. Think carefully about when to draw these weapons, when to shoot, and when to keep them safely tucked away in a hidden holster. Try to avoid feeling anxious, be careful about expressing anger, ask questions to circumvent disappointment and regret, and remember that happiness and excitement can have adverse consequences.

Just as you prepare your tactical and strategic moves before a negotiation, you should invest effort in preparing your emotional approach. It will be time well spent.

Reprinted from Harvard Business Review, *December 2015 (product #R1512C).*

10

Using Mindfulness in Negotiation

by Gaëtan Pellerin

I magine you've just been offered a job and are ready to negotiate your salary. After doing some research around the market value of the role, you overcome your initial apprehension and share your proposal with the hiring manager. You talk through your expectations and make a case for why you deserve to be compensated at the higher end of the range. Everything seems to be going fine until your request is turned down.

How do you feel?

Rejected? Upset? Defensive?

We often perceive negotiations as conversations led by logic. But they are, in fact, very emotional. Emotions are the language of our ego, an unconscious part of our brains that instinctively reacts to external events and that controls a number of our body's vital functions, including our breathing, temperature, and balance.[1] Our ego is respon-sible for our survival—it is what drives our fight-or-fight reactions or the impulses that have historically helped us hunt or avoid being hunted.[2]

While most of us no longer live under constant threat, we do encounter struggles. Our ego may still interpret conflict as a threat, which instinctively puts us in a high-alert mode. This explains why, when a hir-ing manager says no, your ego is triggered, regardless of your experience level. And when this happens, you are more likely to react impulsively and based on neg-ative emotions like fear, self-doubt, anger, resentment, or shame.

Manage Your Emotions During a Negotiation

The good news is that it's possible to change your inter-nal wiring and learn to better manage your emotions by building one skill: mindfulness. Mindfulness involves becoming more aware of your feelings in stressful situa-tions, staying in the present, and moving forward with-out baggage. When you learn how to do this, you will also learn how to gain clarity under stress and let go of your natural ego response.

Like any other skill, mindfulness takes time, effort, and patience to master. Here's a four-step process to get you started.

1. Understand your triggers

High-stress situations, like negotiations, often trigger us psychologically and take us back to moments in our pasts when we experienced similar emotions. These associations are typically driven by our egos but have very little to do with the event we are experiencing in the present. For instance, perhaps as a child, you were rewarded a gold star every time you got a high grade, and so you began to associate hard work with rewards. As an adult, when you don't get the salary you feel you have earned, you may unconsciously recall this experience and feel like a failure, spiraling into negative self-talk about your own worth.[3]

Since associations like this are unconscious, it can be hard to recognize them. Try using the following exercise to figure out what's going on for you internally before your next negotiation:

- What if my manager says no to my request?

- What if they say they dislike my proposal?

- What if my manager is rude or aggressive to me during the negotiation?

For each question, think about how you'd organically react. As you work through the "what-if" scenarios, dig deeper with a couple of follow-up questions:

- What is my go-to response?

- Why do I have this response?

Do your best to be nonjudgmental with yourself as you go through this process. It's going to be emotionally draining, and the self-critical voices in your head will see your vulnerability and want to take over. But the point of this exercise is self-awareness—so be kind to yourself as you work through it.

2. Plan for a different emotional response

Once you have identified your unconscious emotional responses, you can think about how to manage them. It's best to do this before you enter a stressful situation. In the case of negotiations, I suggest asking yourself a few additional questions based on the triggers you identified in the previous step:

- If I feel stuck in the middle of the conversation, what can I do?

- What are some ways to make my case without getting defensive?

- If I hear a no, what are two or three ways to react without feeling frazzled or dejected?

These guiding questions will help you prepare for difficult emotional responses in advance. For example, if you're prone to feeling anxious in situations where you're caught off guard, make a list of all the ways a hiring manager may surprise you and think about how you will respond. If you panic when you sense you're losing the interest of your listener, practice maintaining eye contact or pausing and asking a question to redirect the conversation. You may even consider setting up a mock conversation with a friend to help you identify your stumbles, gain real-time feedback, and hopefully feel at ease.

3. During the conversation, notice your triggers and move on

Even when you've done all the work beforehand, you're still probably going to be triggered at some point during the negotiation process. People are unpredictable, and it's impossible to prepare for every scenario that may come up. That said, there are ways you can respond and move past the difficult moments.

For instance, let's pretend the hiring manager rejects your salary proposal. You notice your palms begin to sweat, your jaws clench, and your heart rate rises. When this happens, pause. Take a deep breath. Inhale for a count of four and exhale for a count of eight. This should help get you out of your own head and restore your body with a sense of calm.

Once you regain composure, think about what you practiced. Instead of letting your triggers threaten you, use them to brainstorm a new way forward. Tap into your creative side and think about how else you can get what you want.

Sticking with this example, don't immediately assume that the hiring manager doesn't value your skills or expertise. Rather, approach the conversation from a place of curiosity. You don't know why the manager said no, so gently nudge them for more information.

Lead with, "Could you help me understand why my request was turned down?" or "I'm curious to understand what part of my request didn't resonate with you?"

You may learn that your salary expectation is outside their salary range for this position. Or maybe they didn't budget for the upper range that you're trying to get. Whatever the reason is, don't hesitate to probe further and fully understand where they're coming from. The more details you gather, the easier it will be to move the conversation forward. In this step, your goal should be to close a deal or get closer to one.

You might, for example, consider that salary is not the only element of compensation. If your hiring manager hasn't budgeted for higher compensation, it may be worth asking for other perks, including travel allowance, a signing bonus, or performance-based rewards. If finances are a top priority, you might also inquire if the company would permit you to take up other freelance opportunities while in the job. Try asking these open-ended questions:

- I would like to renegotiate my salary after six months in this position. What criteria would allow me to renegotiate?

- What is the policy on a signing bonus for this position?

- What is the level required to get stock options as compensation for full-time employees? How can I be eligible for the same?

- What is the company support to pay for an MBA or similar educational perks for their employees?

This creative exercise demonstrates to the employer your ability to pivot and be flexible with your strategy—and the more you practice, the better you get.

Emotions are natural during difficult conversations, but they don't have to sabotage you. Instead, you can plan to lean into whatever you're feeling—take what's useful to you (and others) and leave the rest behind. In the end, you have the agency to decide what to react to, what to embrace, and what to let pass. If you can learn how to do this, you can—and will likely—get closer to what you want.

Adapted from "Managing Your Emotions During a Negotiation," Ascend, on hbr. org, December 7, 2021.

11

The Science of Choking Under Pressure

by Alyson Meister and Maude Lavanchy

Choking under pressure, where one freezes and underperforms when it matters most—even despite deep expertise and years of practice—is well known in the world of sports. But we hear less about the day-to-day chokes that happen at work.

Most of us can reflect on a few of our own choking moments. Maybe you lost your voice or your ability to think straight when speaking with an important client, manager, or audience. Nobody is immune: For example, Mahatma Gandhi had such a moment during his first case before a judge and "ran from the courtroom in humiliation."[1] To help prevent "the choke" at work, we can apply learnings from the world of sports to the world of management.

The Science of Choking Under Pressure

When we "freeze," our bodies are engaging a threat response to something in our external environment. That "something" is different for everyone. At work, it might look like a difficult conversation, a negotiation, a pile of paperwork, or a public speech.

When you choke, physiologically, your body has entered into protection from danger mode and has released a cocktail of stress-related hormones like cortisol and adrenaline. These can elevate your breathing and heart rate, dilate your pupils, and even cause you to sweat. When under threat, your working memory becomes impaired, meaning you have trouble making sense of and acting on new information, become more prone to recalling and reliving negative emotional experiences, and consciously overthink behaviors that should be second nature.[2] Ultimately, when choking, not only does your performance in the moment decline, but it can trigger a vicious cycle of self-doubt, shame, guilt, and fear, making it all the more likely you'll choke again, limit taking future risks, and even suffer long-term mental health consequences, such as the PTSD experienced by Olympic champion René Holten Poulsen.[3]

You're most likely to choke when the external demands or pressure of the situation overwhelm your personal resources to cope with it. This happens, for example, when the stakes are raised and the situation occurs infrequently. While soccer players may find a penalty kick relatively simple during practice, the stakes (for example, your team's entire future and funding) and rarity (that is, you have only this one chance) are immensely elevated in knockout-stage competitions (such as a World Cup final). A choke can also happen even when the pressure remains constant, yet your ability to use coping resources becomes depleted—for example, when you feel anxious or begin to question your abilities. The frustrating part is that this demands-versus-resources imbalance can happen completely unconsciously, meaning that while you think you're ready, your unconscious brain has other ideas.

Face Your Big Moments at Work

Like an athlete ready for the big game, assuming that you've already learned and practiced the skills that you'll draw on, there are a number of techniques that can help you reduce the pressure or boost your ability to cope with it, which will ultimately help you fully access that well-honed skill and both prevent and navigate through a potential choke.[4]

Be there, over and over

Golfing legend Jack Nicklaus famously said, "I never missed a putt in my mind." The same part of the brain is activated when we visualize an action (for example, lifting your left hand) and when we actually perform the action.[5] That's why mental imagery is used to improve motor learning in rehabilitative settings, such as after a stroke.[6]

In the world of sports, star athletes such as Serena Williams, Wayne Rooney, and Michael Jordan are all strong believers in visualization. Visualizing previous successes at crucial moments has multiple benefits: It prepares athletes for various scenarios and allows them to manage expectations and emotions more effectively. There is a significant body of scientific evidence showing the power of visualization to enhance strength, accuracy, and endurance, as well as reducing anxiety and increasing sense of control in emergency situations.[7]

When preparing for a big moment at work, rehearse it in your mind in as much clarity and detail as you can. What will it look and feel like to walk into your manager's office and ask for that raise? How do the lights feel as you walk out in front of the audience, into the boardroom, onto the stage, or even sign on to the videoconference? What will be the first words you say?

Practice for pressure

Athletes train not only for skills and abilities but also for pressure. For the 2012 and 2016 Olympics, Team Great Britain's mental fortitude training gradually increased pressure on athletes to intentionally evoke—and practice working with—their choke response.[8] Top coaches introduce mental, technical, tactical, or physical competitive stressors by unexpectedly changing the usual conditions. For example, they might force right-footed soccer players to use only their left foot during practice or introduce better opponents by surprise. Swimmer Michael Phelps's coach, Bob Bowman, once stepped on and cracked Phelps's goggles before a race, forcing him to compete "blind." This experience proved useful when his goggles filled with water after he dove during an Olympic race in 2008: "From the 150-meter wall to the finish, I couldn't see the wall. I was just hoping I was winning." Not only did he win the gold medal, but he also broke a world record.

Steve Jobs was known for his stellar presentations, but also for the amount of practice he would put in. Rehearsal is important, whether you're alone in your office or in front of a camera or crowd. You can raise the stakes by asking your audience to interrupt you, make a negative comment, or switch off your computer, forcing you to continue without your supporting slides.

Develop a preperformance routine

Those sometimes perplexing routines, movements, or sets of words that you see and hear before an athlete delivers an important serve in tennis, a free throw in basketball, or a penalty kick in soccer have a very important purpose. Rafael Nadal is said to have an elaborate 12-step court routine that lasts around 30 seconds. NBA star Karl Malone was known for his particular free-throw routine that involved speaking to himself.

A preperformance routine can help you clear your mind, get into the moment, and set that well-honed skill to autopilot. At work, you might develop a short ritual, such as breathing exercises, repeating a phrase or mantra, listening to a particular song, sipping a favorite tea, or doing a few physical stretches in your office that can get you in the right mindset to tackle those first moments before autopilot can kick in. Once you've got a routine you're comfortable with, you can use it whenever you need to access the knowledge, skills, and behaviors you've been well trained for. You might also develop a mini-routine that you return to when you realize you're choking.

Don't think, just do

Most athletes know that overthinking in the moment—or paralysis by analysis—can make them doubt themselves or focus too much on every aspect of a movement (for example, the position of your leg and foot when kicking a ball) instead of letting it go (outside of conscious awareness), triggering a choke.[9] To avoid this, some athletes opt for "self-distraction" in the minutes or hours prior to a race or a game. Listening to music, reading, or doing something with your hands to stay out of your head are ways to escape from the surrounding elements and thoughts that could add pressure. For instance, in the minutes before a race, Usain Bolt will randomly think about anything else, until the moment he hears "on your marks." He says: "[N]o matter how much pressure is on, I never think about it, because it starts creeping in and plays with your mind. That's why I clown around before a race. I'm relaxed, I enjoy myself."[10]

Mindfulness and meditation techniques help train you to acknowledge your surroundings while remaining alert, attentive, and present within yourself in the moment. A wealth of research shows how mindfulness and meditation can calm the brain and nervous system, reduce anxiety, and improve performance.[11] Numerous athletes use these techniques before and during big sporting events. For example, Novak Djokovic practices mindfulness daily:

> Instead of trying to silence your mind or find "inner peace," you allow and accept your thoughts as they come. . . . They do bounce around like crazy, but they're supposed to, your job is to let them come and go. . . . I've done so much mindfulness that my brain functions better now automatically. . . . I used to freeze up whenever I made a mistake.

*Now when I blow a serve or shank a backhand, I
still get those flashes of self-doubt but I know how to
handle them.*[12]

Simply writing down your fears can also help alleviate them for performance.[13] Mindfulness trainings are increasingly popular in organizations, and supporting apps have been shown to be effective in reducing performance anxiety (as long as you actually stick to them).

Develop a stress mindset

Tennis legend Billie Jean King has said, "Pressure is a privilege." A decorated champion, King saw stress as "earned." Shifting your mindset from "stress is depleting" to "stress is enhancing" actually changes the way your body responds to it.[14] To do this, next time you're nervous and feel your heart starting to race, don't tell yourself to calm down—your body won't buy it. Rather, tell yourself you're excited and gearing up for optimal performance. Six-time Olympic gold medalist Sir Chris Hoy said, "Never use the words 'nervous' or 'anxious'; use the words 'exciting' and 'adrenalized.'"

When Djokovic is playing in front of a crowd that's mostly in favor of his opponent, he says, "At times you just try to ignore it, which is quite hard, but I like to transmutate it in a way, so when the crowd is chanting 'Roger,'

I hear 'Novak.'" This is a way to tell your body and mind that the stress you're facing is positive, supporting you.

Seemingly small strategies like self-talk (saying "I'm excited" out loud) or inner dialogue telling yourself you're excited can help you harness and channel the stress to focus and perform, averting a choke.[15]

Rationalize the event and your bumps along the way

It's important to put your performance into perspective, so the anticipated results don't overwhelm your ability to perform (or your enjoyment). This involves, for example, disconnecting your identity (that is, who you are as a person) from the results. So a loss doesn't mean that *you* are a loser, and a win doesn't mean that *you* are a winner. For example, after winning gold at the alpine skiing World Cup in 2020, Lara Gut-Behrami said: "It's just a victory, it doesn't change your life. There are more important things." Serena Williams highlights that setbacks are part of the process and motivation to keep going. Prolific basketball coach Dawn Stanley has a 24-hour rule for athletes, whereby they have "24 hours to 'bask in [their] victory' or 'agonize over [their] defeat.'"

You can also put the big moment into perspective by taking what former President Obama refers to as "the long view": reframing any immediate "crises" so that you can see the big picture—whether that's your values or your long-term goals—which can help you minimize the effects and importance of a single event.

. . .

Nobody is immune from choking in a big moment. However, what we learn from the greatest athletes in the world is that there are behaviors and mindsets we can all practice to help prevent a choke and better navigate it when it arrives.

Adapted from content posted on hbr.org, April 7, 2022 (product #H06YV6).

Negotiate Your Role, Responsibilities, and Salary

12

Negotiating as a Woman of Color

by Deepa Purushothaman, Deborah M. Kolb, Hannah Riley Bowles, and Valerie Purdie-Greenaway

N egotiating on your own behalf is hard, and opportunities to do so aren't always obvious, especially if you're not accustomed to feeling empowered. It can also be highly emotional, and you may not even know what your ideal outcome is.

Layered on top of these challenges is an American culture that often discourages women—especially women of color (WOC)—from self-advocating, particularly when it comes to grasping greater power and resources or saying no to undervalued work.[1] In our experience teaching, interviewing, and working with female managers and executives, we commonly hear WOC report feeling an instinct to stay silent and be grateful for what they have. They also often report a reasonable fear of backlash if they strive beyond others' expectations or push back on additional workplace asks.

Negotiating should be seen as a tool to overcome barriers and solve problems; however, many WOC view it as a privilege and often overlook the leverage they have available to them. What can WOC do if they feel cornered into saying yes or feel guilty saying no when what's being asked of them is not in their best interest? Based on our respective work in women's leadership development, including more than 1,000 interviews with professional and executive WOC, *The First, the Few, the Only: How Women of Color Can Redefine Power in Corporate America* (written by one of us), and two decades of research on gender and negotiation, we explore how negotiation tools could help WOC have more agency and be more selective in what they accept—and what they push back on—at work.[2]

Why WOC Don't Negotiate

The WOC we've interviewed did not feel encouraged to negotiate. Many described being coached by others to "go along to get along" for various reasons. Black women found that revealing ambitious intentions and a healthy self-esteem caused them to be misinterpreted as angry, difficult, or aggressive. Many Asian cultures teach a reverence for authority that creates expectations with themselves and others that they should conform. Many immigrant Latinas are cautioned based on family experience not to rock the boat and are taught to keep their heads down.

When these women advance through corporate America, they have few negotiation models tailored toward the unique spaces they occupy. When interviewing WOC, we found that the word "negotiation" often connoted formal, contractual dealmaking. Examples of negotiation that came to mind for these women included job offers or work with clients. This stereotype of negotiation as formal bargaining is typically associated with white male norms. It also overshadows everyday opportunities for WOC to get what they need and want at work (see also chapter 3).

WOC also shared that they worry that advice often offered to white women, such as "lean in" or "just say no," doesn't suit their needs. While white women continue to face barriers at the negotiation table, they may be afforded a broader toolkit of strategies than WOC. Ours and others' research on intersectional invisibility shows that WOC still contend with standing out while also being marginalized.[3] Many receive the message that they're the "exception," implicitly heightening expectations that they conform and don't draw further attention to themselves. The women we met weren't seeing everyday negotiation opportunities in interactions with others around the use of their time, their value, or the spaces they occupy.

We want to model and discuss what WOC might do when asked to take on additional tasks and roles at work—and highlight that there are often choices beyond saying yes or no.

Let's investigate the social and professional positions of women in four different scenarios inspired by our respective research and experience. WOC may find themselves feeling "trapped" in these circumstances, when embracing a negotiation approach could result in better outcomes for the individual WOC, those around her, and her company at large. Our research in the laboratory and field has shown that women can avoid backlash if they have mutually beneficial options and ideas to propose.

The Job-Within-Your-Full-Time-Job Trap

WOC are often asked to take on responsibilities outside the ones they're hired for. The "job within the job"—especially around diversity, equity, and inclusion (DE&I) tasks—is a growing challenge for many of the women we interviewed.

Isabel (not her real name; all names have been changed) is a high-performing marketing manager who has risen rapidly in the advertising field. She is known for speaking her mind, especially when it comes to selling products to Black and Brown markets. As one of the only client-facing people of color in her agency, Isabel has become the voice for diverse customers.

In addition to her regular job duties, she found herself assuming the company's expanding informal DE&I roles. Eventually, one senior leader asked Isabel to take on the DE&I leader role for the San Francisco office. The role itself was very loosely defined and had an unclear job description. Isabel appreciated the way leadership publicly valued her opinions on DE&I questions and was initially excited about the prospect; however, as the conversation progressed, she realized that the opportunity felt like additional work on top of her more than full-time marketing role.

Isabel shared her ambivalence about the position with a close friend, who asked, "Where is the upside?" Isabel explained that she actually enjoys DE&I work, finds it to be personally meaningful, and is very good at it. The work not only is time-consuming, it takes a toll on her well-being. She wondered how much of a difference in her company's culture she could make in the new role and whether it was sustainable for her to add more to her already full plate. And would this work even be rewarded, especially if it distracted her from her marketing responsibilities and the role she was hired and paid to do?

Isabel could negotiate to define the role she wants to play.

If she's interested in the role, Isabel can put a value on the extra DE&I work as a real addition to her current job. One way to do this would be to negotiate with her supervisor about how to prioritize all of her current responsibilities, such as looking for ways to temporarily hand off or back-burner some of her work as she transitions into the new DE&I role.

Isabel might also start a conversation about her time in both roles and the potential implications for her advancement trajectory. While the work would be personally meaningful, it's not the job she was hired to do, and it may not serve her to take her eye off the ball of her marketing strategy. She might also want to explore whether the DE&I role could offer her opportunities to increase her visibility with leadership and negotiate for opportunities that would enhance the visibility of her personal contributions, along with the company's commitment to DE&I.[4]

If the negotiation process reveals that the DE&I work isn't actually highly valued in her firm (for example, they're unwilling to reprioritize her workload or give the work visibility), then she should question whether she's the right—or the only—person for the job. The position should help Isabel *and* her company. If the role is poorly defined and not seen as valuable by leaders, she may want to pass. If she feels the risks of outright saying no are too high, she could use a "yes, and" strategy and negotiate for clear boundaries and expectations around the role in order to avoid mission creep.[5]

The Death-by-a-Thousand-Paper-Cuts Trap

Many of the women we met are among very few WOC in their organizations. As a result, much of the mentoring, sponsoring, and even barrier-breaking responsibility falls on them.

Maria was hired three years ago and has at least 10 peers at her middle management level. Maria finds herself constantly being asked to schedule video calls, send calendar invites, record meetings, and even send out notes afterward. She is one of the few women—and the only WOC—in her department. While she values pitching in for the greater good of the company, she realizes that she's expected to take on far more administrative duties than others.

Maria wants to give back some of these tasks or find a way to share them among the team.

Maria could negotiate for shared responsibility.

It's hard to push back on tasks like this, so Maria may want to schedule a peer meeting to convince her colleagues to share in this work. Maria is not uniquely qualified for this role—there are others who could perform the tasks just as well. She could explain that it's a public good and suggest a rotation or work-share approach since the tasks benefit the entire department.

Once she has buy-in from her peers, the group could propose a new plan to management as a collective. This approach requires coalition-building, working with others to shift the narrative to shared responsibility and shared value.

The Lonely-Only Trap

Maya was recently promoted to her company's C-suite as its new chief strategy officer. Before the promotion, she made mentorship a priority. Now, six months into her new role, she finds herself overwhelmed by the number of women asking to meet with her for coaching and advice. She is the only woman and the only WOC in the C-suite and sees the development of diverse talent as a core strategic objective. Nevertheless, she fears that this ballooning responsibility is starting to edge out other work, mind space, and time she needs to devote to broader strategic initiatives.

She doesn't want to say no to those seeking her advice or complain that mentees are taking up too much of her time. In fact, she really enjoys this part of her new role. Maya wants to be a role model and mentor junior talent without undermining her larger leadership role.

Maya can negotiate to turn individual work into organizational work.

This common type of invisible work often falls on pathbreaking WOC and came up in our interviews frequently.

Maya could explore possibilities to transform her individual and informal mentor role into a formal position within the company. For instance, she could use data on all the requests she receives as evidence for the need of a mentorship program, which she could help develop in concert with talent and human resources teams.

She could argue for making strong mentorship for diverse talent management a competitive advantage for her company. By surfacing this invisible work, she could help others see its hidden value and open doors to conversations about the best use of both the company's and individual contributors' time.

The When-Your-Passion-Isn't-Their-Passion Trap

Dara was on the partner track at her firm. As the only Black woman in a senior role, she found herself tasked with greater DE&I activities. One of the partners even asked her to help shape the firm's inclusion strategy.

After taking a few months to meet with employees, Dara came back with a detailed strategy and execution plan. She presented her recommendations to the leadership team and asked if she could step into a larger, more permanent DE&I leadership role.

Leadership told her that DE&I could be her "minor, not major" and that she was too close to the partner process to risk getting sidetracked by a staff role.

Dara can negotiate to test the market.

Dara's leadership gave her a clear signal of how they value her DE&I contributions relative to her other work. Without negotiating, she could follow their advice and push aside the DE&I work to stay focused on the path to partner.

It may serve Dara to negotiate on two fronts: inside her firm and externally with other companies.

Inside her company, Dara could propose a trial to demonstrate the value of her proposal. She could ask to occupy the position for a short-term stint (90 days or fewer). She could ask for a pilot project and determine the criteria by which it could be judged. Once in the role, she could try to shape the new initiative and a position for herself within it.

Alternatively, she could reject the professional advice she has been given and accept the professional consequences of doing the DE&I work that she finds personally meaningful and important. Dara could also do something more unexpected and ask to come off the partner track altogether. If the role is pivotally important and if Dara is questioning her overall fit within the company and its commitment to DE&I, she may benefit from extending her runway to collect more information.

At the same time, Dara could start exploring what other firms offer by testing her value in the external marketplace. Leaders are sometimes slow to recognize the full value of their internal talent until the market gives them a different signal. She could even use her outside offer to negotiate for what she needs at her current firm.

Having options can strengthen your negotiation position and make you braver about how hard you negotiate. This situation made Dara question how committed the firm was to DE&I and prompted her to think about whether she was in the right place or valued in the ways she should be. Pay attention to these signals in your own professional journey.

The Real Opportunity

Negotiation is a tool for asking for what you want and deserve, bending norms to break open new paths, and shaping new ways of working. Negotiation is not about playing hardball. It's about framing "asks" as opportunities for negotiation and getting creative with options.

Negotiating helps both you and your company. Clarifying expectations for yourself and asking for what you need to be successful helps bring greater clarity about what the company needs and the best way to deploy resources and attention.

When you're asked to do something and don't feel you know what you want yet, it's a good idea to pause. Take the time to gather your thoughts and any relevant information before resuming the discussion. Agency matters. You can't get what you want if you don't know what you want. If you're asked to do something you don't want to do or don't get an answer you like, ask for another meeting and come back with more creative ideas. Sometimes, the outcome of a negotiation is more negotiation.

Here are some powerful negotiation statements you may want to keep handy:

- "Yes, I can do that, but what would I give up?"

- "I will accept this role, but next year, I want to sit on the regional review committee."

- "I have a rule: I never say 'yes' to anything in the moment. I always think about it."

- "I could use your help in understanding how this would make sense for me given my other priorities."

- "If I lead the diversity initiative, how will it be measured for my year-end reviews?"

- "How about I take the role for 90 days and then we revisit it?"

Silence is also powerful, as it prompts others to share more.

If there was ever a time for WOC to negotiate, the moment is now. There's more power available to them in companies than ever before. As they're asked and inspired to do more strategic, emotional, and professional work, they must dedicate more effort to negotiating for themselves and for the generations of leaders to follow. They can use negotiation to reset the tables and set new expectations for their growing roles in organizations.

Adapted from content posted on hbr.org, January 14, 2022 (product #H06SQO).

13

Don't Ask for a Raise—Negotiate It

by Carol Hagh

D oes the thought of asking for a raise or promotion make you nervous? Most people say it does. A recent survey of 3,000 employees in the U.K. revealed that 55% of people are unwilling to ask for a raise.[1] Among the reasons were not knowing what to say (16%), being worried about appearing greedy (15%), or simply being afraid (12%). Whether your nerves stem from fear, low self-confidence, or a lack of knowledge surrounding your market value, asking for more from your employer is uncomfortable—even when the odds are in your favor.

As an executive coach, I've found that taking a step back and approaching these interactions strategically can help calm nerves and increase confidence. One approach that I encourage my clients to practice involves an important principle of negotiation: creating a win-win situation, or what I call a "two-way commitment."

The idea is to first communicate the value you are going to bring to your boss and to your organization, and then discuss what you hope your employer will do for you in exchange. It requires some preparation and a clear understanding of their expectations so that you can make a strong case for yourself and demonstrate your commitment to their success.

Whether you are looking to secure a salary increase, a promotion, a lateral move, more flexibility, or something else that makes you feel valued, respected, and optimistic at work—follow these four steps to put this approach to practice.

Understand the Other Party in the Negotiation

Before going into the negotiation, try to understand your boss's perspective. While a part of their job is to provide you with useful feedback and support your development, they also have multiple, competing priorities—including balancing budgets, meeting business targets, managing your peers, and developing their own career.

You can get a sense of what these priorities are by paying attention to the announcements your company makes about business objectives and asking your manager how your work contributes to those goals. Similarly, make note of what your manager highlights or praises when things are going well and any concerns they express when things are not. These cues may show up during team or one-on-one meetings, or in departmental updates.

Note the work you do that specifically supports the priorities you identify—you can bring these up later, in your negotiation.

Depending on what you want, you should also be aware that your manager may not be the only decision-maker. Often, there are HR guidelines to follow, and for larger requests, your boss may need authorization from *their* boss. For example, let's say you are advocating for a pay raise within the pay band for your role. This is a fairly straightforward request that your manager can probably grant. On the other hand, if you want to be promoted into an entirely new role or transfer teams, that is a much larger request that will require other stakeholders, as well as a review of the head count and budget.

This means that securing a win could sometimes take a significant amount of time. Other times, it may depend on circumstances outside your control. Whatever the case may be, it's important for you to understand these circumstances so that you can be strategic when timing your request. If you know that the company has not been meeting its financial goals, for instance, then this might not be a good time.

Set Your Manager's Expectations Early and Often

The last thing you want to do is surprise your manager with an unexpected request. You can better position yourself for success by bringing up the topic gradually during one-on-one meetings with your boss and gauging their reaction.

I recommend first mentioning what you want in a low-pressure way. If you want a raise, for example, you might start with, "At some point, I'd love for us to talk about my contributions and what I can do to get to the next level," or, "I'd like to discuss my career growth and how I can continue to develop in this role at my next performance review." Your boss's initial response can provide you with a lot of information.

If the reaction is positive, consider it a green light to initiate a more serious discussion down the line. If the reaction is negative, consider it a sign to ask for feedback on your progress or performance. You might ask questions like, "What did you think of the last project I worked on?" "Any advice for what I can do better?" "Do you have any feedback from the team?" or "What's the most important thing for me to work on right now?"

Make sure you listen carefully and incorporate the learnings into your next project before talking again about pay or progression. The more you can learn about what the issue might be, the more effectively you can address it.

At times, you may discover that the issue has nothing to do with you but is related to a budgeting or business challenge. If this is the case, follow up with a question about how much room there will be later on in the year to think about pay and progression. Although it may feel like a sensitive subject, you can do this gracefully by explaining your intentions. For example: "I'm really committed to doing well here, and I can see this isn't the right time for this conversation. What is your sense of how things might look later this year?"

Prepare What You Want and What You Will Offer

When you are ready to have a more formal negotiation, think clearly about what you want. Write down your requests in order of priority. Do you want a higher salary? A new title? A change in reporting line? A bigger budget or team? Which of these is the most important? Are you flexible around the timing on anything? Where can you compromise and where can you not?

Your manager may have more leeway in certain areas than others. For instance, salary may be more difficult to secure than promotions (or vice versa). If you can't get the first item on your list, have a plan B.

Next, think about how you will articulate what you are going to offer in exchange. This is where the "two-way commitment" comes into play. Your employer wants to invest in people who are loyal, enthusiastic, and dedicated to contributing to the success of their company. They do not want to invest in disgruntled employees who are looking for another job or bringing down the morale of their team.

When you're asking for the company to do something for you, it is very important for your commitment to come across in a way that is authentic to you. There are a few ways you can do this:

- Express enthusiasm for where the company is growing.

- Talk about your satisfaction with a recent project that you completed.

- Reiterate how much you care about your teammates.

- Highlight how your work is helping your manager reach their goals.

Through my work, I have heard consistently from organizations that an investable employee is engaged, optimistic, and interested in developing their career and skills. That is the kind of person that companies want to sponsor, develop, retain, and promote. Try to display these characteristics not only in the negotiation but also in your general interactions at work.

Manage the Negotiation

Now you should be ready to talk to your boss. Go into the meeting with an egalitarian "we are both adults" attitude rather than that of a subordinate asking for a favor. If you've done your homework, then you have some insight into what your manager's priorities are, whether they view your performance in a positive light, and how much authority they have to say yes.

It's normal to feel nervous, but a glass of water and some slow, deep breaths can be highly and surprisingly effective should anxiety kick in.

Begin the conversation by reminding your manager that you've been building up to this. You could start by referring to your previous conversations: "I wanted to build on our earlier conversations about my career, as I'm really excited to be here and want to progress," or, "Thank you for the great feedback on Project X. I've learned a lot and I'd like to talk to you about how best to take that forward in my career here." Be sure to mention how committed you are to growing your career *within the company* before diving too deep.

Mention one or two things to highlight specific areas where you've made a big contribution. Then transition into what you want. Be brief and be clear, as a long explanation might sound defensive or argumentative: "It would mean a lot to me to look at my salary and see if the company can support a raise of X," or, "I love working with you and with the team, but I also feel it's time to learn something new and increase my responsibilities. Would you be able to support an internal move/my progression to the next level?"

Once you've made your case, pause to give your manager time to speak. If you have done the right preparation and approached the conversation in a collaborative spirit, you may well hear good news.

Finally, keep in mind that getting what you want at work is a process. Whatever the outcome may be, you will gain insight into your employer's priorities and how you fit within them. You may get exactly what you want, or you may realize that you will need to go elsewhere to do that. The important thing is that you do everything in your control to get the outcome you deserve, and that starts with speaking up for what matters to you.

Adapted from content posted on Ascend, hbr.org, December 2, 2021.

14

Women Ask for Raises as Often as Men but Are Less Likely to Get Them

by Benjamin Artz, Amanda Goodall, and Andrew J. Oswald

t's a concrete fact that women earn less than men do. The true gender pay gap is not known with certainty, but when comparing equally qualified people doing the same job, most labor economists' estimates put it at 10%–20%. The crucial question remains its cause. One common explanation is that women are less likely to negotiate their salaries. We've seen this in both bestselling business memoirs like Sheryl Sandberg's *Lean In* and in previous studies like the research-based book *Women Don't Ask*.

Gaining access to a more recent, and more detailed, data set allowed us to investigate this question anew. What we found contradicts previous research.[1] The bottom line of our study is that women do "ask" just as often as men. They just don't "get."

Even we were surprised by the results. We had expected to find less asking by the women. Instead, we found that, holding background factors constant, women ask for a raise just as often as men, but men are more likely to be successful. Women who asked obtained a raise 15% of the time, while men obtained a pay increase 20% of the time. While that may sound like a modest difference, over a lifetime it really adds up.

We also examined the idea that women act less assertively in negotiations for fear of upsetting the relationship with their boss or colleagues (some evidence for this has been found in previous research).[2] We found no support for this in our data. Instead, we found that although employees do sometimes say that they do not ask for a raise because of concern for their relationships in the workplace, this is equally true of men and women. Both 14% of males and 14% of females say they have done this.

In our project, we examined 4,600 randomly selected employees across 800 workplaces. The sample is from Australia, and the survey was completed in 2014. To our knowledge, it is the only nation with really good information on asking behavior. Although a small country, it arguably has the interesting advantage for our work that it represents a mixture of cultures (with British, Southeast Asian, American, and European influences). Most of the statistical sources that management researchers and labor economists used do not record asking behavior, and do not record people's motivations for refraining from asking. But our data set did have this information. First, the individuals in our data were questioned in detail about their motives, behavior, and histories. Unlike in standard data sources, therefore, it is in principle feasible—admittedly in an imperfect way—to inquire into why women and men choose to act in the ways observed. Second, our data is from matched worker-employer surveys in which random samples of male and female employees can be studied. This is a valuable feature, as it makes it possible to control for many background factors about workplaces that are not observable to the statistical investigator and would be impossible to allow for properly in many conventional statistical sources.

We study answers to survey questions like: "Have you attempted to attain a better wage/salary for yourself since you commenced employment with this employer?" "Were you successful?" and "Why have you not attempted to attain a better wage/promotion for yourself since you commenced your employment? . . . Were you concerned about negative effects on your relationship with your manager/employer?"

As you might guess, lots of different factors do seem to influence the rate of asking. Older workers do so more often. Long-tenured employees do so more often. So do full-timers. Perhaps unsurprisingly, all part-timers, whether male or female, tend both to ask, and to get, less often.

We wondered if we might find a difference by education level. The seminal work by Linda Babcock and Sara Laschever and by Babcock and others examined the behavior of MBA students and found that among that cohort women were less likely to ask.[3] So we wondered: Do elite men ask more than elite women? But when we split our sample of workers into high education and low education, we find no difference between the females and the males. Even when we split those with and without postgraduate degrees, we did not detect significant differences.

We did, however, find intriguing differences across age groups. The younger women in the labor market appear statistically indistinguishable—even in "getting"—from the younger men. Hence it could be that negotiating behavior through the years has begun to change. Future research may be able to decide whether true changes are going on in the modern labor market. Perhaps the world really is beginning to transform.

That is the hopeful explanation for why our findings differ from others. Another is that our data set is based on actual employee behavior, not on laboratory experiments or surveys. (Another is that Australian women may be more likely to ask than women from other countries.) There have been some prior hints in the literature that women's asking behavior is not as different from men's as is commonly described. In a field experiment, Andreas Leibbrandt and John List provide interesting and nuanced results.[4] The authors find no disparity between men and women in the special circumstance that workers are explicitly told that wage negotiation is permitted. When the "rules of wage determination" are left ambiguous, however, Leibbrandt and List conclude that men do tend to negotiate higher pay.

When there is no explicit statement that wages are negotiable, females are more likely than males to signal their willingness to work for a lower wage rate. One earlier study in Great Britain also fails to find evidence to favor a women-don't-ask view.[5] However, it was unable to control for a number of important factors including hours worked or firm size, variables that we were able to include in our study.

When early reports of our work appeared in the press, Sara Laschever and others criticized the research, in part for not having gone through a full peer review. That peer review has now been done.[6] Journal referees were persuaded by our key conclusion, but asked us to do a number of extra checks, and these proved valuable for our case. At the referees' request, after the further analysis, we were able to demonstrate to them that our main finding—women do ask—holds in both large and small companies and holds for women with and without advanced levels of education. We also demonstrated that the finding is not because female workers have shorter lengths of job tenure or behave differently than men when they have dependent children.

Perhaps women have always asked more than they've gotten credit for, and more detailed data just allows us to finally see it. The bottom line is that the patterns we have found are consistent with the idea that women's requests for advancement are treated differently from men's requests. Asking does not mean getting—at least if you are a female.

Adapted from content posted on hbr.org, June 25, 2018, product #H04DEV.

15

Even When Women Ask for a Raise, They Don't Ask for Enough

by Kathryn Heath

Margot, my client, was offered a "great" job as the CFO of a fledgling unit within her company. It was a nice little step up for her, and she was thrilled by the prospect. Margot had earned this promotion by spending the previous six months running her department while her boss was out on leave. She did an exemplary job leading a vast piece of the company and was rewarded with a modest promotion. My first thought? Big whoop, Margot.

In her landmark study, Linda Babcock found that women don't get ahead at work because they don't step up and ask for money and promotions.[1] Our research indicates that this finding still applies, but perhaps not in the way people think. In the process of coaching hundreds of top female executives, we've routinely interviewed hiring managers and pored over 360-degree feedback reports in search of trends and commonalities. One of the things we've found consistently is that women do, in fact, step up and ask for more money and better jobs. But they don't ask for *enough*. They take what they get on their first try

Here's how to lobby for what you really deserve—more.

Raise your expectations

If there are two job openings, why not ask for the dream role rather than the smaller promotion? Always ask for more than you think you deserve in terms of the job and salary level. We've found that women consistently undervalue themselves. They also underestimate where a given position falls in terms of salary range.

Dial it up

Many of the women we coach are worried about being perceived as pushy, when in reality they're not advocating for themselves as forcefully as they should. To help them calibrate their efforts, we tell them to visualize a TV remote—and visualize dialing it up three clicks. That brings the volume up to just about where it needs to be. When it comes to increasing your ask, there is a vast gap between wishy-washy and assertive.

Here's what we mean:

- "I believe I deserve a raise." That's wishy-washy.

- "Based on my work during the acquisition I deserve a [be specific] raise." That's confident.

- "Based on my work managing the team during the acquisition I deserve a [specific] raise and I would like to be put on the fast track for a [be specific] promotion." This is truly assertive.

The best way to dial up an ask is to take credit for your accomplishments and ask for a specific reward that is commensurate—and don't accept anything less.

Ask up the ladder

Research indicates that men are more willing to exchange favors than women are, which puts them in a better position to line up promotions.[2] Women hesitate to trade on their relationships because that feels crass and unseemly. We coach women to network in a much more purposeful way and establish a quid pro quo of career favors with colleagues. In addition, women shouldn't be reticent to network with their boss's boss. Yes, you need to proceed with caution in terms of protocol, but courageously hobnobbing above your level can earn you respect and get you noticed.

Ultimately, this is how Margot got the job she deserved. She did the CFO role well for a few months. During that time, she got to know the division president and told him a little about her experience managing the unit. He was impressed and eventually offered her a much bigger position in the company. It took a lot for someone like Margot (she's modest) to lobby so far above her pay grade, but she did it well, and it paid off in terms of career advancement. And no one thought she was aggressive or overbearing, as she had feared.

In the end, it is important to put things in the proper perspective. There is very little risk—and tremendous reward—in asking for the big job. You will never be considered for it if you don't. And simply stepping up for it means that you are registered for a promotion. Letting people know you want a bigger job is the first step in securing it.

Adapted from content posted on hbr.org, July 14, 2014 (product #H00WIW).

16

Negotiating Your Next Job

by Hannah Riley Bowles and Bobbi Thomason

When we ask professionals to describe a career negotiation, the first thing many people think of is bargaining with a hiring manager over an offer package. That scenario may spring to mind because compensation negotiations can be especially stressful and awkward and therefore become seared into our memories.

Although reaching agreement on pay and benefits is important, failure to think more broadly about your career could mean losing valuable opportunities for advancement. For instance, women are increasingly urged to negotiate for higher pay as a way to close the gender wage gap. However, studies have shown that women's "80 cents on the dollar" is explained more by differences in men's and women's career trajectories than by differential pay for doing the exact same job. Our research and our work coaching executives suggest that negotiating your role (the scope of your authority and your developmental opportunities) is likely to benefit your career more than negotiating your pay and benefits does. And at times of work-life conflict, negotiating your workload and the conditions that affect it (including your responsibilities, your location, and travel requirements) may be critical to remaining gainfully employed and moving forward professionally.

As with other dealmaking, career negotiations should not be solely about getting as much as you can. The best negotiators generate mutually beneficial solutions through joint problem-solving and creative trade-offs, along with compromise. Furthermore, negotiating the direction of your career typically involves multiple stakeholders— including those in your personal life as well as those at work.

We advise professionals to think strategically about not just *what* they might negotiate but *how*. That means going beyond planning what to say at the bargaining table; it requires keeping your eye on larger objectives, ensuring that you are negotiating with the right parties over the right issues, and preventing misunderstandings from derailing your requests or proposals because they are unconventional or potentially pathbreaking.

In the age of Covid-19, the time is ripe to improve your career negotiation skills. Many people are changing how they work (shifting to remote or flexible arrangements, for example), what they are working on (being redeployed or responding to new priorities), and with whom they're working (collaborating in new ways across functions and geographies). And transformations in our work lives are increasingly interlinked with transformations in our personal lives—whether that involves relocation decisions, periods of intense dedication to our jobs, or adapting to spikes in caregiving demands.

Drawing from a research project in which we collected thousands of stories from recent professional-school graduates, mid-level managers, and senior executives from seven global regions about how they advanced at pivotal points in their careers, we propose four steps for preparing for your career negotiations. They progress in a logical order, but you are likely to return to earlier steps as your analysis proceeds. For instance, you might start out intending to negotiate for one type of opportunity but discover that you're better off negotiating for a different type. Or you might initially conceive of a proposal to present to your boss but then come to understand that your boss is actually not the key stakeholder who needs to be persuaded. Particularly for a complex and protracted negotiation, you should continually refine your analysis as you gain information.

1. Start with Your Career Goals

In our experience, negotiators too often start their preparation focused on the opportunity right in front of them, such as a job offer, rather than on their ultimate work and life aspirations. As you enter a period of change in your career, you should think about your short- and long-term aims and then map backward from those objectives to define the next steps you want to take. Don't forget to include quality-of-life considerations as well as professional ones. And be prepared to defer gratification if that's the right thing to do for the endgame.

Anya's story offers a cautionary tale. ("Anya" and all other individuals discussed in this piece are composites of case examples we studied.) When finishing her MBA program, she was evaluating two offers: one in consulting—the field she had previously worked in for several years—and one that would launch a new career in tech, which was what her heart truly desired. (Feeling torn between two industries is common in job searches.) The consulting firm was offering her more money and status than the tech company was—unsurprising, given her track record in consulting and her limited experience in tech (one summer internship). Focused on the terms of the offers, Anya started her negotiation preparation wondering if she should walk away from the tech company unless it matched the salary offered by the consulting firm.

Making compensation the deciding factor can be a mistake. If we'd been coaching Anya, we would have encouraged her to start with her career goal: transitioning out of consulting into tech. We would have encouraged her to compare the competing offers not only with each other but also against her vision of what she wanted to achieve in her first five years out of graduate school. Next, we might have asked, "To improve the tech offer, what might you negotiate to fulfill your dream of a career in tech?" After all, her lifetime earning potential could be higher in that booming sector than in consulting. Perhaps she could accept the lower compensation but negotiate for an accelerated promotion track—a solution that might appeal to the tech company because it would not need to deviate from its compensation standards for MBA recruits.

Such longer-term thinking often pays off. In *Chasing Stars: The Myth of Talent and the Portability of Performance*, Boris Groysberg reports that the financial analysts who were most likely to retain their star status after moving to a new firm were those who had looked beyond pay and carefully researched whether the new firm would provide them with the organizational resources to excel. They understood that being successful in one setting doesn't guarantee success in another, so the compensation package was just one aspect of the job offer to consider. Our advice is to define from the start what you most want to achieve—whether that's being a top professional, making money, or living up to some other ideal—and then keep that goal in mind as your negotiation progresses.

2. Understand What You're Negotiating For

Career negotiations fall into three buckets. In *asking* negotiations, you propose something that's standard for someone in your role or at your level. In *bending* negotiations, you request a personal exception or an unusual arrangement that runs counter to typical organizational practice or norms (for example, a remote work setup or a promotion to a position for which you lack the conventional qualifications). And in *shaping* negotiations, you propose ways to play a role in changing your organizational environment or creating a new initiative (such as revamping the way a project is run or launching a new business unit). Depending on whether you are in an asking, a bending, or a shaping negotiation, you will need to vary your arguments to win your counterparts' support.

In asking situations, you must demonstrate that your request or proposal is reasonable because it fits with existing practices or norms—for example, a pay raise is warranted in light of an outside offer, or you deserve a promotion or a developmental opportunity because other employees with your track record or experience have received such rewards. Asking negotiations often arise in the context of routine conversations about role assignments. If you are asked to do work that would move you away from your career goals, see if there is room for negotiation. For instance, you might be able to explain why the proposed change in your role is not in the employer's interest: Perhaps it would hurt the performance of your team or damage the relationship with a high-value client. Another option is to agree to do the job for the sake of organizational needs in exchange for some other career-advancing opportunity. For example, you might say, "I will take on this role to help us out of the current crisis, but I would like to rotate into a job with more P&L responsibility after two years."

If you are in a bending negotiation—seeking some special exception or privilege—you need to keep your counterparts from doing what's easiest and simply saying, "No, that's not the way things are done around here." Justifying your request is particularly important if you are asking people to take a chance on you, such as putting you in a position for which you are not traditionally qualified.

Consider the case of Bela, who wanted to move from finance into a leadership role in IT as her company launched a digital transformation. The CIO considered her unqualified and seemed likely to dissuade the CEO from giving her the job. Bela came to realize that the CIO wanted someone more experienced to oversee the IT transition, in part because failure would reflect poorly on the CIO's own leadership. So she asked for a six-month trial while the CIO searched for a potential replacement. Bela explained why her deep knowledge of the company's financial systems and her track record managing cross-functional teams prepared her to succeed in this IT role or, at a minimum, keep the company on solid footing until she was replaced by a new hire.

Although any negotiation can backfire, bending negotiations are particularly risky because they may give the impression that you're a prima donna seeking special treatment or unwilling to pay your dues. Deborah Kolb, an expert in career negotiations, suggests a role-play exercise to mitigate this risk: List the reasons why your counterparts would support your proposal; then come up with a list of reasons why they might say no anyway—and your possible responses. Beyond strategizing to get past "no," we advise weighing the downstream career risks and benefits of entering into an exceptional or unconventional work arrangement.

Whereas asking and bending negotiations are focused solely on your personal career path, shaping negotiations center on proposals to change the path of your organization or working group. Because that commonly means seizing leadership opportunities, shaping negotiations typically involve more parties and the backing of allies.

Consider Samir's desire to lead a restructuring of his firm, which was run by an elite old guard that he saw as out of step with globally competitive business practices. Samir recognized that he needed to build a cross-generational coalition to support this change. As he made his case to key colleagues, he found allies among the veteran leaders who recognized that the firm's legacy would depend on retaining bold thinkers like him. He also found peers who appreciated his vision for growth. Finally, with his spouse's support, Samir worked out a plan to relocate internationally for another position if the firm rejected his proposal. He then began the negotiation process with confidence that he had enough buy-in within the firm to lead a transformational change, but also a satisfying alternative for himself and his family if that was not possible.

Organizations may be especially receptive to bending and shaping negotiations during challenging or fast-changing times, when people are looking for ways to adapt and innovate. For instance, in light of the Covid-19 pandemic and social distancing restrictions, many employees need to change the way they work. Their collective bending negotiations are a useful source of information and experimentation for organizations and individuals trying to figure out how to maintain high morale and productivity during the crisis. Organizations are also welcoming shaping proposals from employees who have ideas about how to redeploy resources and open new markets in response to economic disruptions at home and abroad.

3. Reduce Ambiguity About What, How, and with Whom to Negotiate

No one would ever advise walking blind into a potential negotiation, but people do it all the time. One risk is that you'll "get Wahlberged," as the journalist Kate MacArthur put it, writing about how Mark Wahlberg negotiated a payment of $1.5 million to reshoot some scenes in a Hollywood film while his costar Michelle

Williams accepted less than $1,000 for the same work. That case has been highlighted as an example of women's failure to negotiate, but the underlying problem was a lack of information on what was negotiable. Williams had been led to believe that all the actors on the reshoot were effectively donating their time to save the film after another costar was pulled from the cast.

Reducing ambiguity is particularly important for ensuring that people from underrepresented groups—oftentimes women and people of color—get a fair shake. Many organizations are moving to make their recruitment and promotion practices more transparent so that all candidates have access to the same information and opportunities. Increasing transparency is obviously the responsibility of organizations, but individuals can take action too.

As you prepare to negotiate, write down all the questions you have: *What is potentially negotiable? How should I negotiate? Who will be my counterparts, and what do they care about?* There are many sources for this type of information. Talent professionals, for example, will explain in general terms what is typically negotiable and how (although they usually won't reveal the specifics of any individual case). Some information is available online. A media or YouTube search can give you perspective on counterparts' points of view on strategic issues. A LinkedIn search can help you find professional contacts who may tell you more about a hiring manager or a department.

Although your personal and professional networks can be a valuable source of information, you should not rely on them alone to get an unbiased understanding of the situation. Think of a field in which men tend to be better paid than women. If women confer only with other women about customary salaries, and if men confer only with other men, women are likely to enter pay negotiations with lower expectations than men have—and to exit with worse outcomes.

Stretch your inquiry beyond your closest networks to ensure that you have the broadest information possible. Recently many people have been learning from how organizations in other industries or geographies are responding to the challenges presented by the Covid-19 pandemic. Better information helps generate innovative solutions; it can also help you make a persuasive case for managing your career the way you want to during these turbulent times.

4. Enhance Your Negotiations Through Relationships—and Vice Versa

As you aim to reduce ambiguity, you will undoubtedly think of people you might go to for information or advice. You might also think of others who could provide social support—those who would encourage and stand by you and give honest feedback if you are off track. Don't forget to identify potential advocates for your proposal. Who might be willing to speak up in favor of it? Who are your allies? Connecting with people who can be helpful is what we mean by enhancing your negotiations through relationships.

Consider the example of Brandon, an engineer who landed a job as a private equity associate after finishing business school. Lacking finance experience, he had been advised that his prospects of making partner were dim if he did not make a distinctive contribution. Brandon hoped to do that by arguing for the creation of a small fund to invest in marketable robotics projects—an underdeveloped growth area for the firm. Before negotiating to spearhead this initiative, he sought advice from his former robotics professor, who could spot weaknesses in his proposal and help him fix them. He also found a partner at the firm who agreed to let Brandon shadow him on tech company boards.

To build a coalition of support for what you hope to do, you might start off by trying something akin to the shuttle diplomacy used by negotiators of international affairs: Make the rounds of key stakeholders, talking with them individually to solicit their feedback and input. Shuttling is more time-consuming than calling a summit of all interested parties (a meeting to pitch your proposal). But it enables you to privately explore people's interests and concerns and to incorporate their ideas into your game plan. It also helps you predict how people will respond when it comes time for you to present a formal proposal.

If you're concerned that shuttling around might make you appear conniving or manipulative, then be transparent about it. Explain that you're seeking input on an idea you have, and meet early with people who might block your proposal if they felt you weren't consulting them. To broaden buy-in, you might also enlist others to help you get feedback, keeping in mind Harry Truman's words: "It is amazing what you can accomplish if you do not care who gets the credit."

Many of the negotiation cases we studied were rife with tales of conflict and resistance, but you needn't settle for compromises that leave both sides unhappy. The give-and-take that occurs when you're seeking a mutually beneficial deal can open your eyes to other perspectives, help you better understand your colleagues, and find ways of working together to create lasting solutions. In other words, career negotiations can enhance your working relationships—and we encourage you to strive for that outcome.

To generate goodwill and motivate agreement, we recommend that you explain to counterparts both why it is legitimate for you to be negotiating and how your proposal takes their interests into account. That's not always easy. For instance, we met one female executive who found out for the second time that a male subordinate was being paid more than she was. She probably wanted to say many things to senior leaders at her firm, but she chose the approach she knew would be most persuasive: "I know you are going to want to fix this, because it is inconsistent with company practices and values."

Or take the example of Sandra, who ran the U.S. division of a major business unit and wanted to globalize it. To achieve her aim, she had to make a strategic case for why globalization was in the company's best interest and why she was the right person to lead the initiative. Addressing the hopes and concerns of managers both at headquarters and in the non-U.S. business units required numerous rounds of conversation in which she seeded and got feedback on her ideas. Sandra told us: "Over time, the logic [for globalization and my leadership] became compelling."

. . .

The four steps outlined above take time to implement—and there will be false starts and reversals. Most of the career negotiations recounted to us by senior executives, managers, and other professionals lasted weeks or months. They started with preliminary conversations that gradually evolved, particularly as new information or the entrance of new players influenced the way various parties perceived their interests and the alternatives to agreement.

To maximize your odds of success, set targets for yourself that are specific and realistic—and that help hold you accountable to follow through with your plan amid pressing distractions and demands. Too often, negotiations fizzle or never get off the ground because larger goals become buried by everyday work.

One senior executive we interviewed told us, "You have a book to write of your life. Don't let anyone else write your chapters." We second that, but we also urge you to remember that great careers are not authored alone. Your narrative will be cowritten with work and life partners, and negotiation is at the heart of finding mutually gratifying ways for that story to unfold.

Reprinted from Harvard Business Review, *January–February 2021 (product #R2101E).*

NOTES

Chapter 1

1. Benjamin Artz, Amanda Goodall, and Andrew J. Oswald, "Research: Women Ask for Raises as Often as Men, but Are Less Likely to Get Them," hbr.org, June 25, 2018, https://hbr.org/2018/06 /research-women-ask-for-raises-as-often-as-men-but-are-less-likely -to-get-them.

2. Beverly DeMarr and Suzanne C. de Janasz, *Negotiation and Dispute Resolution*, 2nd ed. (Chicago: Chicago Business Press, 2019).

3. Linda Babcock and Sara Laschever, *Women Don't Ask: The High Cost of Avoiding Negotiation—and Positive Strategies for Change* (New York: Bantam, 2007).

4. Hannah Riley Bowles, Linda Babcock, and Lei Lai, "Social Incentives for Gender Differences in the Propensity to Initiate Negotiations: Sometimes It Does Hurt to Ask," *Organizational Behavior and Human Decision Processes* 103, no. 1 (2007): 84–103.

5. Roger Fisher and William L. Ury, *Getting to Yes: Negotiating Agreement Without Giving In* (New York: Penguin, 2011).

6. Lisa A. Barron, "Ask and You Shall Receive? Gender Differences in Negotiators' Beliefs About Requests for a Higher Salary," *Human Relations* 56, no. 6 (June 2003): 635–662.

7. John Buelow, "3 Benefits of Making Role-Play Part of Training," *Training*, February 6, 2014, https://trainingmag.com/3-benefits -of-making-role-play-part-of-training/.

8. Joseph P. Forgas, "On Feeling Good and Getting Your Way: Mood Effects on Negotiator Cognition and Bargaining Strategies," *Journal of Personality and Social Psychology* 74, no. 3 (1998): 565–577.

9. Cameron Anderson and Leigh L. Thompson, "Affect from the Top Down: How Powerful Individuals' Positive Affect Shapes Negotiations," *Organizational Behavior and Human Decision Processes* 95, no. 2 (2004): 125–139.

10. Peter J. D. Carnevale and Alice M. Isen, "The Influence of Positive Affect and Visual Access on the Discovery of Integrative Solutions in Bilateral Negotiation," *Organizational Behavior and Human Decision Processes* 37, no. 1 (1986): 1–13.

11. Tanis Bryan and James Bryan, "Positive Mood and Math Performance," *Journal of Learning Disabilities* 24, no. 8 (October 1991): 490–494.

12. Rimma Teper, Zindel V. Segal, and Michael Inzlich, "Inside the Mindful Mind: How Mindfulness Enhances Emotion Regulation Through Improvements in Executive Control," *Current Directions in Psychological Science* 22, no. 6 (December 2013): 449–454.

13. Babcock and Laschever, *Women Don't Ask.*

14. Gaëlle Desbordes et al., "Effects of Mindful-Attention and Compassion Meditation Training on Amygdala Response to Emotional Stimuli in an Ordinary, Non-Meditative State," *Frontiers in Human Neuroscience* 6 (2012), doi.10.3389/fnhum .2012.00292.

15. Emily T. Amanatullah and Catherine H. Tinsley, "Punishing Female Negotiators for Asserting Too Much . . . or Not Enough: Exploring Why Advocacy Moderates Backlash Against Assertive Female Negotiators," *Organizational Behavior and Human Decision Processes* 120, no. 1 (2013): 110–122.

16. Hannah Riley Bowles, "Constraints and Triggers: Situational Mechanics of Gender in Negotiation," *Journal of Personality and Social Psychology* 89, no. 6 (n.d.): 951–965.

17. Hannah Riley Bowles, "Why Women Don't Negotiate Their Job Offers," hbr.org, June 19, 2014, https://hbr.org/2014/06 /why-women-dont-negotiate-their-job-offers.

Chapter 3

1. Linda Babcock and Sara Laschever, *Women Don't Ask: The High Cost of Avoiding Negotiation—and Positive Strategies for Change* (New York: Bantam, 2007).

Chapter 4

1. Carol T. Kulik, Ruchi Sinha, and Mara Olekalns, "Women-focused Negotiation Training: A Gendered Solution to a Gendered Problem," in *Research Handbook on Gender and Negotiation*, ed. Mara Olekalns and Jessica A. Kennedy (Cheltenham, UK: Edward Elgar, 2020), 297–326.

2. Emily T. Amanatullah and Catherine H. Tinsley, "Punishing Female Negotiators for Asserting Too Much . . . or Not Enough: Exploring Why Advocacy Moderates Backlash Against Assertive Female Negotiators," *Organizational Behavior and Human Decision Processes* 120, no. 1 (2013): 110–122.

3. Katharina G. Kugler et al., "Gender Differences in the Initiation of Negotiations: A Meta-analysis," *Psychological Bulletin* 144, no. 2 (2018): 198–222.

4. Kulik, Sinha, and Olekalns, "Women-focused Negotiation Training."

5. Hannah Riley Bowles, Linda Babcock, and Lei Lai, "Social Incentives for Gender Differences in the Propensity to Initiate Negotiations: Sometimes It Does Hurt to Ask," *Organizational Behavior and Human Decision Processes* 103, no. 1 (2007): 84–103.

6. Carol T. Kulik and Mara Olekalns, "Negotiating the Gender Divide: Lessons from the Negotiation and Organizational Behavior Literatures," *Journal of Management* 38, no. 4 (July 2012): 1387–1415.

7. Catherine H. Tinsley et al., "Women at the Bargaining Table: Pitfalls and Prospects," *Negotiation Journal* 25 (2009): 233–248.

8. Emily T. Amanatullah and Michael W. Morris, "Negotiating Gender Roles: Gender Differences in Assertive Negotiating Are Mediated by Women's Fear of Backlash and Attenuated When Negotiating on Behalf of Others," *Journal of Personality and Social Psychology* 98, no. 2 (2010): 256–267.

9. Julie K. Norem and Edward C. Chang, "The Positive Psychology of Negative Thinking," *Journal of Clinical Psychology* 58 (2002): 993–1001; Alison Wood Brooks, "Get Excited: Reappraising Pre-performance Anxiety as Excitement," *Journal of Experimental Psychology* 143, no. 3 (2014): 1144–1158.

10. Daniel L. Shapiro, "Negotiating Emotions," *Conflict Resolution Quarterly* 20 (2002): 67–82.

11. Ethan Kross, Ozlem Ayduk, and Walter Mischel, "When Asking 'Why' Does Not Hurt: Distinguishing Rumination from Reflective Processing of Negative Emotions," *Psychological Science* 16, no. 9 (September 2005): 709–715.

12. Daniel L. Shapiro, "Teaching Students How to Use Emotions as They Negotiate," *Negotiation Journal* 22 (2006): 105–109.

13. Benjamin Lewis et al., "See the Benefit: Adversity Appraisal and Subjective Value in Negotiation," *Negotiation Journal* 34 (2018): 379–400.

14. Deborah M. Kolb, "Staying in the Game or Changing It: An Analysis of *Moves* and *Turns* in Negotiation," *Negotiation Journal* 20 (2004): 253–268.

15. Benjamin Artz, Amanda H. Goodall, and Andrew J. Oswald, "Do Women Ask?," *Industrial Relations* 57 (2018): 611–636.

16. Hannah Riley Bowles, Bobbi Thomason, and Julia B. Bear, "Reconceptualizing What and How Women Negotiate for Career Advancement," *Academy of Management Journal* 62 (2019): 1645–1671.

17. Mara Olekalns, Brianna Barker Caza, and Timothy J. Vogus, "Gradual Drifts, Abrupt Shocks: From Relationship Fractures to Relational Resilience," *Academy of Management Annals* 14 (2020): 1–28.

Chapter 5

1. Sue Shellenbarger, "The Mistakes You Make in a Meeting's First Milliseconds," *Wall Street Journal*, January 30, 2018, https://www.wsj.com/articles/the-mistakes-you-make-in-a-meetings-first-milliseconds-1517322312.

2. Elizabeth Blankespoor, Bradley E. Hendricks, and Gregory S. Miller, "Perceptions and Price: Evidence from CEO Presentations at IPO Roadshows," *Entrepreneurship and Finance eJournal*, 2015.

3. Sarah Jessen and Tobias Grossmann, "Unconscious Discrimination of Social Cues from Eye Whites in Infants," *Journal of the Proceedings of the National Academy of Sciences* 111, no. 45 (2014): 16208–16213.

4. Nicole Torres, "When You Pitch an Idea, Gestures Matter More Than Words," *Harvard Business Review*, May–June 2019, https://hbr.org/2019/05/when-you-pitch-an-idea-gestures-matter-more-than-words.

5. Leadership Signals, "Top Gestures," The UK Domain, n.d., https://www.theukdomain.uk/leadership-signals/#/gestures.

6. Noah Zandan, "How to Stop Saying 'Um,' 'Ah,' and 'You Know,'" hbr.org, August 1, 2018, https://hbr.org/2018/08/how-to-stop-saying-um-ah-and-you-know.

7. Dom Barnard, "Average Speaking Rate and Words per Minute, *Virtual Speech*, January 20, 2018, https://virtualspeech.com/blog/average-speaking-rate-words-per-minute.

8. Barnard, "Average Speaking Rate and Words per Minute."

Chapter 6

1. Alice F. Stuhlmacher and Maryalice Citera, "Hostile Behavior and Profit in Virtual Negotiation: A Meta-Analysis," *Journal of Business and Psychology* 20 (2005): 69–93.

2. Boris B. Baltes et al., "Computer-Mediated Communication and Group Decision Making: A Meta-analysis," *Organizational Behavior and Human Decision Processes* 87, no. 1 (2002): 156–179.

3. Guido Hertel et al., "Do Shy People Prefer to Send E-mail?: Personality Effects on Communication Media Preferences in Threatening and Nonthreatening Situations," *Social Psychology* 39, no. 4 (2008): 231–243.

4. Justin Kruger et al., "Egocentrism Over E-mail: Can We Communicate as Well as We Think?," *Journal of Personality and Social Psychology* 89, no. 6 (2005): 925–936.

5. Christoph Laubert and Jennifer Parlamis, "Are You Angry (Happy, Sad) or Aren't You? Emotion Detection Difficulty in Email Negotiation," *Group Decision and Negotiation* 28, no. 2 (April 2019): 377–413.

6. Alice F. Stuhlmacher, Maryalice Citera, and Toni Willis, "Gender Differences in Virtual Negotiation: Theory and Research," *Sex Roles: A Journal of Research* 57, no. 5–6 (2007): 329–339.

7. Aparna Krishnan, Terri R. Kurtzberg, and Charles E. Naquin, "The Curse of the Smartphone: Electronic Multitasking in Negotiations," *Negotiation Journal* 30, no. 2 (2014): 191–208.

8. Charles E. Naquin and Gaylen D. Paulson, "Online Bargaining and Interpersonal Trust," *Journal of Applied Psychology* 88, no. 1 (2003): 113–210.

9. Michael Morris et al., "Schmooze or Lose: Social Friction and Lubrication in E-mail Negotiations," *Group Dynamics: Theory, Research, and Practice* 6, no. 1 (2002): 89–100.

10. Terri R. Kurtzberg, Charles E. Naquin, and Liuba Y. Belkin, "Humor as a Relationship-Building Tool in Online Negotiations," *International Journal of Conflict Management* 20, no. 4 (2009): 377–397.

11. Steven J. Heine et al., "Mirrors in the Head: Cultural Variation in Objective Self-awareness," *Personality and Social Psychology Bulletin* 34, no. 7 (2008): 879–887.

Chapter 7

1. Dacher Keltner, Deborah H. Gruenfeld, and Cameron Anderson, "Power, Approach, and Inhibition," *Psychological Review* 110, no. 2 (2003): 265–284.

2. Leigh L. Thompson, Jiunwen Wang, and Brian C. Gunia, "Negotiation," *Annual Review of Psychology* 61 (2010): 491–515.

3. Richard M. Emerson, "Power-Dependence Relations," *American Sociological Review* 27, no. 1 (1962): 31–41.

4. Rebecca J. Wolfe and Kathleen L. McGinn, "Perceived Relative Power and Its Influence on Negotiations," *Group Decision and Negotiation* 14 (2005): 3–20, https://doi.org/10.1007/s10726-005-3873-8.

5. Susan T. Fiske, "Controlling Other People: The Impact of Power on Stereotyping," *American Psychologist* 48, no. 6 (1993): 621–628.

6. Program on Negotiation Staff, "BATNA and Other Sources of Power at the Negotiation Table: 3 Sources of Power Negotiators Can Use at the Bargaining Table," Harvard Law School, March 29, 2022, https://www.pon.harvard.edu/daily/batna/negotiation-skills-three -sources-of-power-at-the-bargaining-table/.

Chapter 10

1. Stan Rodski, *The Neuroscience of Mindfulness: The Astonishing Science Behind How Everyday Hobbies Help You Relax* (New York: HarperCollins, 2019).

2. "Understanding the Stress Response," Harvard Health Publishing, Harvard Medical School, July 6, 2020, https://www.health .harvard.edu/staying-healthy/understanding-the-stress-response.

3. Andrew S. Fox et al., eds., *The Nature of Emotion: Fundamental Questions* (Series in Affective Science) 2nd ed. (Oxford, UK: Oxford University Press, 2018).

Chapter 11

1. Scott Stossel, "Performance Anxiety in Great Performers: What Hugh Grant, Gandhi, and Thomas Jefferson Have in Common," *Atlantic*, January/February 2014, https://www.theatlantic.com /magazine/archive/2014/01/what-hugh-grant-gandhi-and-thomas -jefferson-have-common/355853/.

2. Luethi Mathias, Meier Beat, and Sandi Carmen, "Stress Effects on Working Memory, Explicit Memory, and Implicit Memory for Neutral and Emotional Stimuli in Healthy Men," *Frontiers in Behavioral Neuroscience* 2 (2009), doi: 10.3389/neuro.08.005.2008.

3. Michael J. Mannor et al. "Heavy Lies the Crown? How Job Anxiety Affects Top Executive Decision Making in Gain and Loss Contexts," *Strategic Management Journal* 37 (2016): 1968–1989.

4. Sian Beilock and Thomas Carr, "On the Fragility of Skilled Performance: What Governs Choking Under Pressure?" *Journal of Experimental Psychology* 130 (2002): 701–725.

Notes

5. David Breitling, Wilfried Guenther, and P. Rondot, "Motor Responses Measured by Brain Electrical Activity Mapping," *Behavioral Neuroscience* 100, no. 1 (1986): 104–116.

6. Carolee J. Winstein et al., "Guidelines for Adult Stroke Rehabilitation and Recovery: A Guideline for Healthcare Professionals from the American Heart Association/American Stroke Association," *Stroke* 47, no. 6 (2016): e98–e169.

7. Deborah L. Feltz and Daniel M. Landers, "The Effects of Mental Practice on Motor Skill Learning and Performance: A Meta-analysis," in *Essential Readings in Sport and Exercise Psychology,* Dajiel Smith and Michael Bar-Eli, eds. (Champaign, IL: Human Kinetics, 2007), 219–230.

8. David Fletcher and Mustafa Sarkar, "Mental Fortitude Training: An Evidence-based Approach to Developing Psychological Resilience for Sustained Success," *Journal of Sport Psychology in Action* 7, no. 3 (2016): 135–157.

9. Sian L. Beilock et al., "When Paying Attention Becomes Counterproductive: Impact of Divided versus Skill-focused Attention on Novice and Experienced Performance of Sensorimotor Skills," *Journal of Experimental Psychology: Applied* 8, no. 1 (2002): 6–16.

10. Decca Aitkenhead, "Usain Bolt: 'I Feel Good Because I Know I've Done It Clean,'" *Guardian*, November 12, 2016, https://www .theguardian.com/sport/2016/nov/12/usain-bolt-feel-good-because -know-done-it-clean.

11. Yi-Yuan Tang et al, "Central and Autonomic Nervous System Interaction Is Altered by Short-term Meditation," *Proceedings of the National Academy of Sciences of the United States of America* 106, no. 22 (2009): 8865–8870; Darren J. Good et al., "Contemplating Mindfulness at Work: An Integrative Review," *Journal of Management* 42, no. 1 (January 2016): 114–142.

12. Novak Djokovic, *Serve to Win: The 14-Day Gluten-free Plan for Physical and Mental Excellence* (New York: Penguin, 2014).

13. Sara Reardon, "Want to Ace Your Test? Share Your Feelings," *Science*, January 13, 2011, https://www.science.org/content/article /want-ace-your-test-share-your-feelings.

14. Alia J. Crum et al., "The Role of Stress Mindset in Shaping Cognitive, Emotional, and Physiological Responses to Challenging and Threatening Stress," *Anxiety, Stress, and Coping* 30, no. 4 (2017): 379–395.

15. Alison Wood Brooks, "Get Excited: Reappraising Preperformance Anxiety as Excitement," *Journal of Experimental Psychology: General* 143, no. 3 (2014): 1144–1158.

Chapter 12

1. Hannah Riley Bowles, Linda Babcock, and Lei Lai, "Social Incentives for Gender Differences in the Propensity to Initiate Negotiations: Sometimes It Does Hurt to Ask," *Organizational Behavior and Human Decision Processes* 103, no. 1 (2007): 84–103; Madeline E. Heilman and Julie J. Chen, "Same Behavior, Different Consequences: Reactions to Men's and Women's Altruistic Citizenship Behavior," *Journal of Applied Psychology* 90, no. 3 (2005): 431–441.

2. "PowHER Redefined: Women of Color Reimagining the World of Work," https://www.powherredefined.com/.

3. Valerie Purdie-Vaughns and Richard P. Eibach, "Intersectional Invisibility: The Distinctive Advantages and Disadvantages of Multiple Subordinate-Group Identities," *Sex Roles* 59 (2008): 377–391.

4. Alexis Nicole Smith et al., "Making the Invisible Visible: Paradoxical Effects of Intersectional Invisibility on the Career Experiences of Executive Black Women," *Academy of Management Journal* 62 (2019): 1705–1734.

5. Deborah Kolb, "A Short Course from Howard Raiffa," *Negotiation Journal* 33 (2017): 333–335; Deborah M. Kolb and Jessica L. Porter, *Negotiating at Work: Turn Small Wins into Big Gains* (Hoboken, NJ: Jossey-Bass, 2015).

Chapter 13

1. Francis Churchill, "More Than One in 10 Workers 'Too Scared' to Ask for a Pay Rise," *People Management*, May 2, 2019, https://www .peoplemanagement.co.uk/article/1742348/more-than-one-in-ten -workers-too-scared-ask-for-pay-rise.

Chapter 14

1. Benjamin Artz, Amanda H. Goodall, and Andrew J. Oswald, "Do Women Ask?," *Industrial Relations* 57 (2018): 611–636.

2. Emily T. Amanatullah and Michael W. Morris, "Negotiating Gender Roles: Gender Differences in Assertive Negotiating Are Mediated by Women's Fear of Backlash and Attenuated When Negotiating on Behalf of Others," *Journal of Personality and Social Psychology* 98, no. 2 (2010): 256–267.

3. Linda Babcock and Sara Laschever, *Women Don't Ask: Negotiation and the Gender Divide* (Princeton, NJ: Princeton University Press, 2003); Linda Babcock and Sara Laschever, *Ask for It: How Women Can Use the Power of Negotiation to Get What They Really Want* (New York: Penguin, 2009); and Linda Babcock et al., "Gender Differences in the Propensity to Initiate Negotiations," in *Social Psychology and Economics*, David De Cremer, Marcel Zeelenberg, and J. Keith Murnighan, eds. (Mahwah, NJ: Lawrence Erlbaum Associates Publishers, 2006), 239–259.

4. Andreas Leibbrandt and John A. List, "Do Women Avoid Salary Negotiations? Evidence from a Large-scale Natural Field Experiment," *Management Science* 61, no. 9 (2015): 2016–2024.

5. Patrick McGovern et al., *Market, Class, and Employment* (Oxford, UK: Oxford University Press, 2008).

6. Artz, Goodall, and Oswald, "Do Women Ask?"

Chapter 15

1. Linda Babcock and Sara Laschever, *Women Don't Ask: The High Cost of Avoiding Negotiation—and Positive Strategies for Change* (New York: Bantam, 2007).

2. Sylvia Ann Hewlett, "The Sponsor Effect: Breaking Through the Last Glass Ceiling," hbr.org, January 12, 2011, https://store.hbr .org/product/the-sponsor-effect-breaking-through-the-last-glass -ceiling/10428.

INDEX

administrative duties, asked of
women of color, 125–126
agency, 105, 120, 130
aggression, 8, 9, 32, 39, 40, 44,
66, 120
alternatives, in negotiations,
16–18
ambiguity, reducing, in
negotiations, 159–161
amygdala, 7
anger
See also emotions
vs. anxiety, 82
disappointment and, 92
displaying, in negotiations, 42,
78–79, 80
faking, 87–88
managing, 41, 43, 86–91
anticipatory anxiety, 42
anxiety, 19–20, 80, 102–103
See also emotions
vs. anger, 82
anticipatory, 42

avoiding, 82–86
reducing, 7, 16, 43, 113–114
Artz, Benjamin, 141–146
Asian cultures, 120
See also women of color
asking negotiations, 155–157
assertiveness, 20–23, 40, 41, 142,
148–149

Babcock, Linda, xiii, 144, 147
bargaining
formal, 121
at stores, 30–31
BATNA (best alternative to a
negotiated agreement),
61–67
bending negotiations, 155–158,
159
bias, fixed-pie, 86–87
Black women. *See* women of
color
body language, 47, 48–49

177

Discussion Guide

Since the *Women at Work* podcast first launched, we've heard from people all over the world that it has inspired discussions and listening groups. We hope that this book does the same—that you'll want to share what you've learned with others. The questions in this discussion guide will help you talk about the challenges women face in the workplace and how we can work together to overcome them.

You don't need to have read the book from start to finish to participate. To get the most out of your discussion, think about the size of your group. A big group has the advantage of spreading ideas more widely—whether throughout your organization or among your friends and peers—but might lose some of the honesty and connection a small group would have. You may want to assign someone to lead the discussion to ensure that all participants are included, especially if some attendees are joining virtually. And it's a good idea to establish ground rules around privacy and confidentiality. *Women at Work* topics touch on difficult issues surrounding sexism and racism, so consider using trigger warnings.

Finally, think about what you want to accomplish in your discussion. Do you want to create a network of mutual support?

Hope to disrupt the status quo? Or are you simply looking for an empathetic ear? With your goals in mind, use the questions that follow to advance the conversation about women at work.

1. How do you define negotiation? Do you consider it to be a term that only applies to formal situations, such as contracts, job offers, and the like? Or do you feel it also includes informal and sometimes interpersonal situations such as dividing household labor with a partner or roommate, or trying to get your toddler out the door in the morning?

2. What low-stakes opportunities do you see to practice your dealmaking skills so that you feel more confident and competent when approaching high-stakes negotiations?

3. In chapter 2, small-business owner Marisa Mauro mentioned that she baked pies to get ready for a negotiation. How do you prepare for a negotiation? Do you rehearse with a partner or colleague, give yourself a pep talk in the mirror, or create and complete checklists?

4. Strong emotions are an expected and manageable part of any deal—not something to suppress or avoid. What sorts of emotions do you typically experience during a negotiation? Do you tend to blow up? Ramble on nervously beyond your prepared points? Or retreat? What emotions make you uncomfortable when your counterpart displays them? How might you

change or expand your mindset to understand and use emotions more effectively in the room?

5. What are your negotiation triggers? When someone hits a nerve, what is your go-to response? Why do you think you have this response? What steps do you or could you take to neutralize your trigger(s) in the future?

6. How important to you is the location and context of your meeting? Do you feel more comfortable face-to-face where it can be easier to read the room, body language, and the like? Or do you feel more confident on-screen, with ready access to your notes and the ability to keep your nervous leg kick off-screen? What are some of the pros and cons of virtual versus in-person negotiations?

7. In what way might you reframe not knowing how a deal will play out from something unsettling to something with potential? In addition to asking yourself *What don't I know that I need to know?*, how can you express curiosity and learn more about your counterpart, their business, and their wants and needs?

8. Consider a time a negotiation didn't work out the way you wanted it to. Why do you think it didn't turn out well? Did your messaging or positioning miss the mark? Were your alternatives too few or too narrow? If you were to replay that negotiation now that you know more, what would you do differently?

9. For ongoing partnerships, how has your relationship with your counterpart been affected by the outcome of your negotiation(s)? Do you feel your relationship is stronger or weaker? If you've had a contentious conversation, what steps did you take to reset the relationship? Have you ever experienced a relationship that was irreparably damaged—or unexpectedly strengthened—after a negotiation?

10. When it comes to asking for what you want on the job, which aspect do you struggle with the most: Garnering resources for your team? Securing professional development opportunities or career advancement for yourself? Asking for accommodations around work-life balance or a health issue? If family or feelings are a factor, is it difficult to frame your request in the context of the business?

11. Consider areas where you don't mind asking for more. What could you draw from that to apply to areas where you struggle? For instance, do you find it easier to make big asks on behalf of others? What can you use from those negotiations in your individual asks?

12. Have you attempted to negotiate a better salary, new title, or increased responsibilities in your current job? If so, were you successful? What do you think contributed to that success? Would you do anything differently (like dialing up your ask by three clicks of

the remote, as mentioned in chapter 15)? If you haven't asked, what barriers stand in your way?

13. Chapter 12 provides several powerful negotiation statements for readers to keep handy, like "Yes, I can do that, but what would I give up?" Which statements in this chapter resonated most with you? Think about a time when you were successful in a negotiation. Were there statements—or pauses or pacing—that you used that you could add to your library of go-to language to use in a future negotiation?

14. How do you take care of yourself after a negotiation? Do you review the process, and your role in it, celebrating successes and noting things you'd do differently? Do you talk it out with a trusted colleague?

15. After reading this book and participating in this discussion group, name one step you'll take to prepare, conduct, and learn from your next negotiation:

- Short term: tomorrow

- Longer term: this month

- Longest term: this year

ABOUT THE CONTRIBUTORS

Amy Gallo, *Women at Work* **cohost,** is a contributing editor at *Harvard Business Review* and the author of *Getting Along: How to Work with Anyone (Even Difficult People)* and the *HBR Guide to Dealing with Conflict* (both Harvard Business Review Press, 2022 and 2017, respectively). She writes and speaks about workplace dynamics. Watch her TEDx talk on conflict and follow her on Twitter @amyegallo.

Benjamin Artz is a professor at the University of Wisconsin at Oshkosh.

Hannah Riley Bowles is the Roy E. Larsen Senior Lecturer in Public Policy and Management at Harvard Kennedy School, where she codirects the Center for Public Leadership and Women and Public Policy Program. She has won awards for her teaching and research on the role of negotiation in women's leadership advancement.

Alison Wood Brooks is the O'Brien Associate Professor of Business Administration at Harvard Business School.

Beth Cabrera is the author of *Beyond Happy: Women, Work, and Well-Being*. As a writer, researcher, and speaker, she helps individuals achieve greater success and well-being. Her leadership development programs focus on positive culture, strengths, meaning, mindfulness, and workplace well-being.

Suzanne de Janasz is a professor of management and conflict resolution (a joint appointment) at George Mason University and a consultant to dozens of organizations. For the past 25 years, she's been teaching negotiation and leadership on five continents, including programs she's designed specifically for women and executives, and those in contracts, real estate, defense/intelligence, consulting, and manufacturing. In addition to publishing dozens of practitioner articles on negotiation, de Janasz is a coauthor of *Negotiation and Dispute Resolution*, now in its second edition.

Carmine Gallo is a Harvard University instructor, keynote speaker, and author of 10 books translated into 40 languages. Gallo is the author of *The Bezos Blueprint: Communication Secrets of the World's Greatest Salesman*.

Amanda Goodall is a reader at Bayes Business School.

Carol Hagh is the founder of Old Game New Rules, which provides executive coaching and leadership development services to corporate clients. She is on the board of directors at Chesnara, a UK-based, publicly listed insurance and pension company. She was previously with the executive search firm Spencer Stuart, where she placed key executive and nonexecutive directors, worked with boards on leadership succession, and published on leadership and talent management. Carol lives in London and is a working parent with two children.

Kathryn Heath is a managing director at Bravanti. She is a coauthor of *I Wish I'd Known This: 6 Career-Accelerating Secrets for Women Leaders*.

Jay A. Hewlin is the president and CEO of the Hewlin Group, a network of attorneys and organizational development scholars. Jay's specialties include employment law, leadership, conflict resolution, negotiations, and DEI. Jay is a lecturer in law at Columbia Law School, where he teaches a negotiation workshop, and is a lecturer for McGill University's Executive Leadership Institute.

Deborah M. Kolb is the Deloitte Ellen Gabriel Professor for Women and Leadership (emerita) at Simmons University and former executive director at the Harvard Program on Negotiation. She is the author of several award-winning books, including *The Shadow Negotiation: How Women*

Can Manage the Hidden Agendas That Determine Bargaining Success and *Negotiating at Work.*

Carol T. Kulik is a research professor of human resource management at the University of South Australia, UniSA Business. Her research investigates how disadvantaged employees can negotiate employment arrangements that benefit both parties in the employment relationship.

Maude Lavanchy is a research fellow at IMD Business School in Lausanne, Switzerland, and a semiprofessional volleyball player. Passionate about sports, economics, and new technologies, her research is part of the field of economics and organizational behavior. Her thought leadership has been covered by the popular press and media, including Bloomberg, World Economic Forum, *Fortune*, Quartz, *Forbes India*, Channel News Asia, and *Ouest-France*.

Marisa Mauro is the owner and operator of Ploughgate Creamery at Bragg Farm, in Vermont.

Alyson Meister is a professor of leadership and organizational behavior at IMD Business School in Lausanne, Switzerland. Specializing in the development of globally oriented, adaptive, and inclusive organizations, she has worked with thousands of executives, teams, and organizations spanning professional services through to industrial goods and technology. In 2021, she was recognized as a Thinkers50 Radar thought leader. She has recently joined the Scientific Advisory Board for OneMind at Work, focusing on advancing mental health in the workplace. Follow her on Twitter @alymeister.

Hal Movius is a psychologist who helps leaders and organizations negotiate more effectively and confidently. Founder of Movius Consulting, he is the author of two acclaimed books, *Resolve* and *Built to Win*, and consults for leading organizations around the world.

Carolyn O'Hara is a writer and editor based in New York City. She's worked at the *Week, PBS NewsHour,* and *Foreign Policy.*

Mara Olekalns is a professor of management (negotiations) at the Melbourne Business School at the University of Melbourne. Her research explores how negotiators can build relational resilience and overcome adversity in negotiation.

Andrew J. Oswald is a professor of economics and behavioral science at the University of Warwick.

Gaëtan Pellerin has spent the last 10 years as a negotiation consultant-coach, helping negotiators hone their skills and prepare and rehearse for their upcoming live deals. He is the author of *Mindful NEGOtiation: Becoming More Aware in the Moment, Conquering Your Ego and Getting Everyone What They Really Want.*

Valerie Purdie-Greenaway is an associate professor of psychology at Columbia University and teaches negotiations at Columbia Business School. Her groundbreaking research on intersectional invisibility has been widely cited and used by companies to foster inclusive workplaces.

Deepa Purushothaman is the cofounder of nFormation, which provides a brave, safe, new space for professional women of color, and a Women and Public Policy Program Leader in Practice at the Harvard Kennedy School. She is also the author of *The First, the Few, the Only: How Women of Color Can Redefine Power in Corporate America*.

Ashleigh Shelby Rosette is a dean and management professor at Duke University's Fuqua School of Business.

Ruchi Sinha is an associate professor of organizational behavior at the University of South Australia, UniSA Business. Her research explores how voice, conflict, and power dynamics influence work relationships and performance outcomes.

Bobbi Thomason is an assistant professor of applied behavioral science at Pepperdine Graziadio Business School. Follow her on Twitter @bobbithomason.

Women *at* Work
Inspiring conversations, advancing together

ABOUT THE PODCAST

Women face gender discrimination throughout our careers. It doesn't have to derail our ambitions—but how do we prepare to deal with it? There's no workplace orientation session about narrowing the wage gap, standing up to interrupting male colleagues, or taking on many other issues we encounter at work. So HBR staffers Amy Bernstein and Amy Gallo are untangling some of the knottiest problems. They interview experts on gender, tell stories about their own experiences, and give lots of practical advice to help you succeed in spite of the obstacles.

Listen and subscribe:

Apple Podcasts, Google Podcasts, Spotify, RSS

Inspiring conversations, advancing together

  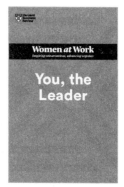

Based on the HBR podcast of the same name, **HBR's Women at Work series** spotlights the real challenges and opportunities women face throughout their careers—and provides inspiration and advice on today's most important workplace topics.